The
Lavender
Cookbook

The
Lavender
Cookbook

by Sharon Shipley

RUNNING PRESS
PHILADELPHIA · LONDON

9   8   7   6   5   4
Digit on the right indicates the number of this printing

Library of Congress Control Number: 2003095209

ISBN-10: 0-7624-1830-3
ISBN-13: 978-0-7624-1830-5

Interior illustrations by Sophie Allport
Cover and interior design by Alicia Freile
Edited by Jean Rogers
Typography: MrsEaves and Univers

This book may be ordered by mail from the publisher.
Please include $2.50 for postage and handling.
But try your bookstore first!

Running Press Book Publishers
125 South Twenty-second Street
Philadelphia, Pennsylvania 19103-4399

Visit us on the web!
www.runningpress.com

I dedicate this book

to my grandmother Laura Rogers, who gave me the love of just-picked garden fruits, vegetables, and flowers

to my Belgian grandmother, Irma Henry, who gave me the passion for food and preserving the history and memories of old recipes

. . . and finally to my late good friend Doris McCarthy, who gave me the encouragement to pursue writing this cookbook. She told me that anything is possible and that I should go and do it.

ACKNOWLEDGMENTS

Many individuals have helped me shape this book by discussing ideas and sources and providing encouragement for cooking with lavender. Several of these people I owe a special thank you.

Ty Kaprelian: who put in many hours of developing my ideas and testing and proofreading all of the recipes for this book.

The pastry chefs at Mon Chéri Cooking School: for testing all of the pastry recipes again and again.

Donna Boehm: who also spent many hours of eyestrain proofreading for me.

Susan Ditz of Rancho Alegre Lavender Farm: who believed in this project from the beginning and offered technical suggestions on growing, harvesting, and cooking with lavender buds.

My friend, cookbook author and freelance writer, Peggy Fallon: for providing excellent professional advice on the recipes in the book.

Of course to all of my family, friends, and staff at Mon Chéri, who tasted all of the lavender recipes. And to my students who have taken the Cooking with Lavender classes: for their valuable feedback and interest.

To my culinary colleagues who encouraged me to write this book: Shirley Corriher, Nathalie Dupree, Marilyn Harris, Carmen Jones, and Blake Swihart. And to Maureen McKeon, who took me to Lavandula Lavender Farm in Australia.

Many thanks to Lisa Croll for organizing my trips to Provence. She helped me capture the magic of Provence.

Special gratitude to my editor, Jean Rogers, for her support, patience, insight, and encouragement with the lavender book.

I would also like to give a special acknowledgment to Lisa Ekus, my agent, for her hard work, perseverance, and belief in a cooking with lavender book.

FOREWORD

"In the Alpes-de-Haute in Provence on a warm June day . . . wandering high in the mountains above the little village of Moustiers . . . I came upon fields of purple lavender, carpeting the hillsides and filling the air with a sweet scent." As Sharon Shipley transports you to these magnificent mountains, you can almost smell the faint scent of lavender. And you too begin to have an intense longing for the rich, yet delicate lavender scent of the foods of Moustiers.

Recently, I had a delicious pork dish that I loved. The predominant flavor was delicate, intriguing, and elusive. I couldn't identify it. I had to know what it was. To my amazement, the chef explained that the marvelous flavor was lavender. I thought that I knew the taste of lavender, but obviously I did not.

I was confusing taste with the familiar scent of lavender that has perfumed my life for as long as I can remember—from fragrant oils and sachets to precious jars of lavender-studded herbes de Provence. Cooking with lavender has always held a certain mystique . . . some secret alchemy.

When I read the first few sentences of *The Lavender Cookbook*, I was hooked; I could not put the book down. I started reading the recipes, and I knew that I was in the presence of a master. Apricot-Lavender Chicken on a Bed of Apples, Dried Apricots, and Pecans—that sounds wonderful! I can imagine the toasted pecans with a little sweet, crisp apple and just a sliver of dried apricot, and all with a bite of perfectly cooked, delicately flavored lavender-apricot chicken breast. Then there's Grilled Lavender Seafood Salad with Pacific Rim Dressing. And Lavender Lemon Pork Chops with Caramelized Pears. What a great combination: pork with caramelized pears.

Sharon's recipes are creative without being overly complex. The novice cook will delight in this collection. Until now, a dessert garnished with a lavender sprig or a lavender-infused beverage was considered quite exotic. Sharon teaches how to incorporate lavender into entertaining menus as well as everyday meals and points out how lavender can elevate the flavor of so many old favorites.

Recipes run the gamut from picture-perfect appetizers and beverages to soups, salads, side dishes, entrées, and, of course, beloved desserts such as Honey Lavender Pound Cake with White Chocolate Drizzle. One of my favorite pound cakes is similar, and when I think about adding honey and lavender and icing the deep golden-brown, deliciously moist cake with white chocolate—oh my!

It is no wonder that Sharon makes sensational-looking, incredibly delicious food. Mon Chéri, her catering company, is one of the best anywhere. She was awarded the "1998 Award of Excellence" by the International Association of Culinary Professionals. She catered a large party for a U.S. president and his guests, with separate menus for the Secret Service and the press. For years, she has been the preferred caterer for Silicon Valley companies. Her outstanding recipes reflect the knowledge of years of experience and consistent excellence in a very competitive field.

In addition to these breathtakingly beautiful, creative recipes, Sharon Shipley gives you complete information, including seed suppliers, on how to grow your own lavender plants, even in large pots. Lavender is a hardy perennial herb, a member of the mint family. Once established, it tolerates extremes such as hot, dry summers and very cold winters, so it can grow most anywhere.

Harvesting and drying instructions are also included, with exactly how to tell when to harvest (timing is everything when cutting lavender). Properly harvested and dried, lavender buds stored in dark blue or amber glass can maintain their flavor for several years.

This is the most comprehensive lavender cookbook to be published. I think that, like me, you will refer to it whenever you want to make your meals more flavorful.

Shirley O. Corriher, CCP
Author of *CookWise: The Secrets of Cooking Revealed*

CONTENTS

PROVENCE AT YOUR DOORSTEP

My love affair with lavender began in the Alpes-de-Haute in Provence on a warm June day back in 1992. Wandering high in the mountains above the little village of Moustiers, near the Gorges du Verdon, I came upon fields of purple lavender, carpeting the hillsides and filling the air with a sweet scent. That experience sparked my passion to learn all there is to know about this magical herb.

The lure of the lavender fields still draws me back to Haute-Provence year after year to inhale the heady aroma. The scent of lavender permeates the air as billows of steam escape the lavender distillers while this precious sun-colored oil is extracted from delicate purple buds. Autumn's morning sun bathes the harvested fields and the fragrant drying sheds in rich gold. Winter's stark beauty soon arrives. Downy white snowflakes gently blanket the hardy lavender plants, while the whistling mistral winds blow through sparkling white rows. Winter passes into spring, awakening the lavender soon to emerge and carpeting the hillsides with velvety sage-green growth.

It is essential when traveling through Provence to visit the plentiful and lavish farmers' markets that reflect the culinary specialties of each region. Having traveled and taught in Provence for many years, I always bring students to these lush outdoor food markets. Within the aisles, you find an amazing array of lavender products, from honey and tea to goat cheese and bottled lavender essence. Therein you will find the exquisite regional Moustiers faïence pottery and beautiful table linens, both decorated with the lavender sprays motif. These memories of Haute-Provence create an intense longing for the rich, yet delicate lavender redolence found in this region's cooking.

Lavender, or what the French call "blue gold," has grown wild throughout the Mediterranean for millennia. Historians indicate that since the days of the Roman Empire, lavender's distinctively scented flowers have been gathered for their healing and soothing properties as well as for use as a culinary herb. Queen Elizabeth I of England was known to favor lavender in cooking and used lavender tea for treatment of severe migraine headaches.

Yet only since the 1920s has lavender production become commercialized and the dried flowers available in America.

Sweet and savory, the delicate scent of lavender enlivens food dishes with its fresh enticing flavor. Many people have experienced lavender only in the classic herbes de Provence mixture, but there are many more uses for this versatile herb. In this book, you'll learn how to infuse your food with the delectable essence of the tiny lavender flower.

My friend Susan Ditz is owner of Rancho Alegre Lavender in Pescadero, California. She not only grows lavender by the acre but teaches classes on its cultivation. She's as knowledgeable as they get, and I'm indebted to her for the information that follows.

Cultivating Lavender for the Kitchen

You needn't grow lavender to reap its culinary benefits. But if you do plant your own, you'll be doubly rewarded.

Although is it unclear where lavender actually originated (some say Persia, Egypt, Italy, Greece, or Spain), it grows wild in the chalky dry ravines of the French Sea Alps, where the conditions may be harsh. Most of the lavender available today has adapted to withstand a lot of variations in weather. English Lavender, known as *Lavandula angustifolia officinalis* (also known also as True Lavender or Vera), and *L. x intermedia* 'Provence' (a hybrid) tolerate extremes such as hot, dry summers and very cold, snowy winters as long as the roots don't stay wet for more than a few days.

A perennial herb that can flourish more than a decade, lavender produces dozens of fragrant blossoms on a single plant in late spring and summer. As a bonus, depending on growing conditions, a second, less abundant bloom may take place in the fall.

Although some chefs prefer to use *angustifolia*, the lower camphor and resin content of 'Provence' makes it the most appealing culinary lavender. Delicate, fresh lavender flower petals are prized for desserts. Dried stems of other varieties with more robust scents and higher oil content, such as *L. x intermedia* 'Grosso', are sometimes used to produce savory lavender smoke on the grill.

Cultivating lavender for culinary use is fairly easy, even for the novice gardener. Two elements are essential for success: plenty of sun and good drainage. A healthy lavender plant has deep, spreading roots. The optimal growing medium is sandy loam and a pH of 7.0. The plant head needs to be above the soil line.

Most commercial farmers add some form of calcium around the plants each fall to improve the pH balance and break up the soil. For heavy clay soil, the remedy is to dig down at least 2 feet, amend with well-decomposed organic material, and then turn the soil over. Avoid using pig and chicken manure, which may burn plants. Another trick is to plant on mounds or sloping hillsides to increase drainage.

Although planting directly in soil is preferable, the more compact varieties ('Munstead', 'Blue Cushion', and 'Hidcote' are popular) will do well in deep, wide pots. However, the life span and amount of foliage will be reduced.

While lavender is considered drought tolerant when mature, new plants need regular watering until they are established. If planted in climates with moderate spring and summer rainfall, they will need less. Drip irrigation is preferable because overhead sprinkling can promote fungal disease. If the planting area tends to be windy, a little more water may be necessary.

Good weed control is essential for robust blooming. Mulch can be useful for small planting areas. But keep it away from the main plant stem. Too much mulch may promote water retention and root rot.

Another key to maintaining healthy vigorous plants is proper pruning. If you plant in spring or summer, pinch off all emerging flowers until the following spring to put energy into the root system. Each year after flowering, cut back one-third to one-half of the plant, about an inch above where the wood begins. This pruning may seem drastic, but it is critical. Always prune or harvest plants with sterilized tools to avoid contamination.

Lavender is very appealing to humans, but generally deer, moles, and voles won't bother with it. Rabbits, however, may dig up small plants to nibble the roots. Lavender is also generally disease resistant.

Bees are attracted in large numbers by the fragrant flowers, and they help in pollination. Many beekeepers place hives in a lavender field to produce honey that is highly prized for its delicate flavor. Don't worry about ladybugs nesting in the lavender branches. They are beneficial in keeping out insects such as aphids that may spread disease from other plants in nearby gardens.

Harvesting and Drying Lavender

Timing is everything when cutting lavender. Plants are ready for harvesting when the bottom third of the flower head (known as a spike) is blooming. This magic window of time varies from garden to garden, depending on an array of circumstances, including annual rainfall, temperature variations, and ratio of overcast to sunny days. Look carefully at each plant daily, because not every stem is ready to be cut at the same time. Having only a few plants affords the opportunity to do very selective cutting.

Before you start your harvest, make sure the sun has dried the morning dew off the spikes. Grasp a handful of lavender stems down close to the foliage and chop the bundle, using sharp, sterilized shears or a Japanese scythe.

Lavender stays fresh for about 3 days in water. Keep cuttings out of the sunlight. Change the water and trim the stems daily. When you desire fresh petals, pick the spikes and use the flowers immediately. The tiny lavender flowers dry quickly once removed from the flower head.

For drying lavender, remove all the foliage from the stems and bundle about an inch or so from the base of the stems with a rubber band. There should be no more than 100 stems in a bundle so air can move around the flowers and prevent the growth of mildew.

Hang the bundles upside down in a dark, dry place with plenty of air circulation. Put a clean cloth underneath to catch any buds that may fall. Darkness preserves the rich color of the flower heads. For drying a few bundles, an infrequently used closet works well.

To hang bundles, use a bent paper clip, placing one side through the rubber band and slipping the other end over a wire coat hanger. A small oscillating fan can help move air around more efficiently. The lavender will be dry in about 8 to 10 days.

To separate buds from stems, rub flower heads gently between your hands over a clean cloth or plate. If necessary, sift flower heads through a sieve to remove dried bracts (tiny leaves at the base of buds). Store lavender buds in a dark blue or amber glass container out of the light. The buds should maintain their flavor for several years if handled this way.

Hint #1: Use the dried stems as grilling sticks to add a smoky lavender flavor to meat, poultry, and fish. Soak the stems in water for 5 minutes before placing on the grill.

Hint #2: If you grind lavender buds in a spice grinder, you release more essential oil. This can increase the lavender flavor in recipes.

For best results: The recipes in this book were developed using dried culinary 'Provence' lavender buds. It has a very low camphor level, a nice floral note, and a gentle lavender flavor. Other varieties of lavender can taste perfumey, bitter, and medicinal.

To ensure your cooking success, please make an effort to find 'Provence' culinary lavender. If you can't locate any in your area, see the resources guide at the back of the book for mail-order sources.

BRING LAVENDER

TO THE TABLE

CONTENTS

It's easy to incorporate lavender into your everyday cooking. Start by simply grinding a small amount of the flower buds and adding them to your favorite recipes. You'll give new dimension to everything from steamed vegetables to cookie dough. But don't stop there. Branch out to new dishes, like the ones in this book.

Some of my recipes call for lavender seasoning mixes or flavored sweeteners. You could certainly make them as needed, but you'll save a little time—and be more apt to extend the flavor of lavender to other foods—if you prepare these basic items ahead.

Lavender Salt Dry Rub

Use this mixture to season meat and seafood, including whole chickens and ducks, pork chops and loins, and fish fillets. Generously rub it into the meat, wrap in plastic, and refrigerate for about 3 hours before cooking.

Interestingly, this lavender salt is also perfect for rimming margarita glasses. See the Lavender Margaritas recipe on page 74.

Store unused rub in a tightly sealed jar in a cool, dark place. It keeps well for 3 months, with the lavender flavor slowly diminishing after that.

MAKES ¹/₂ CUP

1 tablespoon culinary 'Provence' lavender buds
¹/₂ cup coarse sea salt

In a spice grinder, pulse the lavender until finely ground. Transfer to a small bowl and toss with the salt.

Lavender Salt Wet Rub

Like their dry counterparts, wet rubs are an effective seasoning agent. Just massage them into any meat before baking, broiling, or grilling.

This lavender mixture is especially good on roasted whole chicken and pork loin as well as grilled skin-on chicken breasts. Rub a generous amount all over the meat, cover, and refrigerate for 1 to 3 hours or even overnight. The longer you leave it on, the more flavor will be infused into the meat.

You can easily double this recipe. Store any leftover rub in a sealed container in the refrigerator, where it will keep for 5 days.

MAKES ABOUT ¹/₂ CUP

2 teaspoons dried culinary 'Provence' lavender buds
2 tablespoons coarse sea salt
2 tablespoons extra-virgin olive oil
2 tablespoons finely chopped garlic
1 teaspoon fresh rosemary leaves, finely chopped

In a spice grinder, pulse the lavender with 1 tablespoon of the salt until finely ground. Transfer to a small bowl and stir in the oil, garlic, rosemary, and the remaining 1 tablespoon salt.

SPICED LAVENDER SEASONING

This is my favorite seasoning. I rub it on everything, including ribs, chicken, and halibut. The combination of lavender and freshly toasted spices makes this very versatile and simply delicious.

When you're looking for a dazzling hostess or holiday gift, whip up a batch or two of this mix. Package it in small, clear jars to show off its pretty brick-red color. Be sure to include a label with suggested uses.

Store the seasoning in an airtight container in a cool, dark place for up to 2 months.

MAKES ABOUT ½ CUP

2 tablespoons cumin seeds
1 tablespoon coriander seeds
2 tablespoons dried culinary
    'Provence' lavender buds
2 tablespoons dried thyme leaves
2 tablespoons achiote rojo
    seasoning paste (see note)
1 tablespoon freshly ground
    black pepper
½ teaspoon fine sea salt

Toast the cumin and coriander seeds in a dry skillet over medium heat until fragrant, about 2 minutes. Transfer to a spice grinder and add the lavender. Pulse until finely ground. Transfer to a food processor and add the thyme, seasoning paste, pepper, and salt. Pulse to create a homogenous mixture.

Achiote rojo paste is a dry blend of exotic spices that uses the annatto seed as its main ingredient. It can be found in most Mexican supermarkets and may go under the name of annatto seed paste. I like El Mexicano brand.

LAVENDER SUGAR

Oh, what great lavender flavor this gives baked goods! I like sprinkling it on scones, muffins, and even shortbread before baking. (And it's the perfect quick fix when you forget to add lavender to the batter or dough.) I also like how the lavender gives the sugar a gentle kiss of color that's especially evident on light-colored desserts such as sugar cookies.

But don't reserve this sugar just for baking. Use it to sweeten lemonade and other beverages for really easy and impressive drinks. By all means, make up jars of this for your friends.

The sugar easily keeps for a year, but the lavender flavor will slowly diminish after 6 or 7 months.

MAKES 2 CUPS

1 tablespoon dried culinary 'Provence' lavender buds

2 cups granulated sugar

In a spice grinder, pulse the lavender with 1 tablespoon of the sugar until finely ground. Transfer to a bowl and stir in the remaining sugar. Transfer to a jar, cover tightly, and let stand for at least 3 days before using.

LAVENDER VANILLA SUGAR

I really like the combination of lavender and vanilla. It's great for most any sweetened baked good. Add it right to the batter or simply sprinkle some over the top before baking.

When the recipe calls for a fair amount of sugar, use half plain and half flavored so it's not overpowering. Try this blend in your next batch of sugar cookies and I think you'll be quite impressed with yourself.

The sugar is best used within 1 month.

MAKES 2 CUPS

2 cups granulated sugar

2 vanilla beans, cut in half lengthwise and then into small pieces (see note)

1 tablespoon dried culinary 'Provence' lavender buds

In a spice grinder, pulse 2 tablespoons of the sugar with the vanilla beans until very finely minced. Transfer to a bowl. In the spice grinder, pulse the lavender with 1 tablespoon of the remaining sugar until finely ground. Transfer to the bowl and stir in the remaining sugar. Transfer to a jar, cover tightly, and let stand for at least 5 days before using.

If you don't have vanilla beans, use 1 teaspoon vanilla powder, which is available in most upscale supermarkets and cooking stores. Don't use vanilla extract, because the liquid will cause the sugar to clump and discolor.

Lavender Powdered Sugar

This powdered sugar is strictly for flavor and drama. Sprinkle it on top of desserts to decorate and subtly flavor them. As you bite into a daintily dusted dessert, a whisper of the sugar remains on your top lip. When you lick your lips, you again experience sweet lavender rapture.

The sugar is best used within 1 month.

MAKES 2 CUPS

2 cups confectioners' sugar
**1 tablespoon dried culinary
'Provence' lavender buds**

In a spice grinder, pulse 2 tablespoons of the sugar with the lavender until finely ground. Transfer to a bowl and stir in the remaining sugar. Transfer to a jar, cover tightly, and let stand for at least 5 days before using.

Lavender Syrup

The sky's the limit to what this syrup can transform. I add it to martinis, white wine coolers, lemonade, iced tea, and more.

Many mixed drinks call for "simple syrup." That's a fancy name for sugar dissolved in water. Just replace it with lavender syrup. You can convert other drinks to lavender aperitifs by adding the syrup to taste. For lavender martinis, for example, add 1 tablespoon of lavender syrup. For something like lemonade, replace a portion of the sugar with syrup.

Store the syrup for up to 2 weeks in the refrigerator.

MAKES 1 ³/₄ CUPS

1 cup water
1 cup sugar
**2 tablespoons fresh or dried culinary
'Provence' lavender buds**
1 small strip lemon zest

In a small saucepan, boil the water and sugar for a few minutes until the sugar dissolves. Remove from the heat and stir in the lavender and lemon zest. Steep for 20 minutes. Strain into a container with a tight-fitting lid and refrigerate until needed.

LAVENDER BUTTER

With its complement of honey and lavender, this butter makes a great partner to muffins, scones, and even sweet cornbread.

You can form the butter into a log, as I suggest below, and slice off coins as needed. Or you can use a cookie press to extrude pretty shapes onto parchment or wax paper. Put in the freezer until solid, peel off the paper, and store the dabs in freezer bags. When company comes, take out a few pieces and let them come to room temperature.

Frozen, the butter stays fresh-tasting for about a month. In the refrigerator, it keeps for about a week.

MAKES ¼ POUND

¼ pound (1 stick) unsalted butter,
    at room temperature
1 tablespoon honey or lavender
    honey
1 tablespoon dried culinary
    'Provence' lavender buds, finely
    ground in a spice grinder

Place the butter, honey, and lavender in the bowl of a food processor. Pulse until just combined. Transfer to a sheet of parchment or wax paper. Roll into a 1-inch-wide log. Refrigerate or freeze.

LAVENDER CRÈME FRAÎCHE

Crème fraîche is a rich, thickened cream with a slightly tangy flavor. It can be used as a substitute for sour cream and has the advantage that it will not curdle when added to hot liquids, such as soups and sauces. It's also a nice alternative to whipped cream. With the addition of lavender, it's a wonderful complement to desserts and even soups (try Asparagus Soup with Lavender Lemon Cream on page 34).

You can buy plain crème fraîche, but it tends to be expensive and isn't available in many stores. It is, however, really easy to make. The basic technique is the same whether you add lavender or not.

MAKES ABOUT 1 CUP

1 cup heavy cream
    (not ultrapasteurized)
2 tablespoons buttermilk
1 teaspoon dried culinary
    'Provence' lavender buds, finely
    ground in a spice grinder

Combine the cream and buttermilk in a glass bowl. Cover loosely with plastic wrap and let stand at room temperature (65° to 70°F) for 8 to 24 hours, or until very thick. Stir in the lavender. Cover tightly and refrigerate overnight before using. Store in the refrigerator for up to 10 days.

PRESERVED LAVENDER LEMONS

Preserved lemons have been steeped in a salty solution until their texture is silken and their flavor distinctive. They are one of my favorite ways to add pizzazz to salad dressings, pasta, and main courses of all sorts. You need only a little bit to dramatically enhance almost any dish.

They're expensive in gourmet stores, but they're really easy to make. And by doing so, you can give them that little extra je ne sais quoi: *lavender.*

These make a great gift, especially if you layer the lemon wedges in a beautiful glass jar so the yellow skins face outward.

MAKES ABOUT 2 QUARTS

8 large lemons
^{2}/$_3$ cup coarse sea salt
^{1}/$_3$ cup sugar
3 tablespoons minced garlic
**2 tablespoons dried culinary
  'Provence' lavender buds**
Extra-virgin olive oil

Bring a large saucepan of water to a boil over high heat. Prick the skins of the lemons five or six times with a fork. Add to the saucepan and boil for 5 minutes. Drain and set aside until cool enough to handle. Cut the lemons lengthwise into quarters.

In a small bowl, mix the salt, sugar, garlic, and lavender. Start layering the lemon wedges in a widemouthed 2- or 3-quart glass or porcelain jar. Sprinkle each layer lightly with the salt mixture. Press down lightly on the lemons and pour in enough olive oil to cover them by 1/2 inch. Cover securely and refrigerate at least 3 days or up to 1 month before using. Store in the refrigerator.

SPRING LAVENDER

Fresh and Enlivening

CONTENTS

Spicy Duck Empanadas
with Blackberry Citrus Dipping Sauce

Rich flavors of port, duck, and cinnamon infuse these mini party favorites, and the fruity dipping sauce complements the spicy filling. The easy cream cheese dough is very versatile, so you can use it with other savory or even sweet mixtures.

MAKES 24 TO 30 EMPANADAS

Cream Cheese Dough
    (recipe follows)
2 duck breast halves, trimmed of fat
¹⁄₂ cup port wine
3 tablespoons unsalted butter
1 small red onion, minced
¹⁄₄ pound button mushrooms,
    finely chopped
¹⁄₄ cup beef broth
¹⁄₄ cup mashed roasted garlic
    (see note)
1 teaspoon ground cinnamon
1 teaspoon dried culinary
    'Provence' lavender buds, finely
    ground in a spice grinder
¹⁄₂ teaspoon crushed hot-pepper
    flakes
¹⁄₄ cup fresh cilantro leaves,
    finely chopped
1 large egg
1 tablespoon heavy cream
Blackberry Citrus Dipping Sauce
    (recipe follows)

Prepare the dough and refrigerate for 1 hour.

Cut a round of parchment paper to fit inside a large skillet. Set aside.

Place the skillet over medium heat for 3 minutes, until hot. Add the duck breasts and sauté for 2 minutes, or until lightly browned. Turn the breasts over and add the port. Cook for 5 to 10 minutes, or until the meat is cooked through (cut with a sharp knife to test); as the breasts cook, spoon the liquid over them to glaze them. Transfer the breasts to paper towels and set aside until cool enough to handle. Cut into a fine dice.

Wipe out the skillet with paper towels. Add the butter and melt over medium-high heat. Add the onion and sauté for 3 minutes, or until translucent.

Add the mushrooms. Reduce the heat to medium and place the parchment on top of the mushrooms. Cook for 5 to 10 minutes, or until the mushrooms release their liquid and the liquid then reduces to about 1 tablespoon. Remove the parchment.

Stir in the broth, garlic, cinnamon, lavender, and pepper flakes. Cook, stirring, until the broth cooks away. Remove from the heat, let cool to room temperature, and stir in the cilantro.

Preheat the oven to 350°F. Line 2 baking sheets with parchment paper.

On a lightly floured surface, roll one piece of dough until ¹⁄₈ inch thick. Using a 3-inch round cookie cutter, cut out as many rounds as possible. Reserve the dough scraps, combine into a ball, roll again, and cut more rounds. Only roll the scraps once.

Beat the egg and cream together in a cup. Brush the edges of each round with some of the egg mixture. Scoop a rounded tablespoonful of cooled filling onto half of each round and fold the other half over the filling.

Press the edges to seal tightly and brush with the egg mixture. Transfer the rounds to a baking sheet. Repeat to use the remaining dough, filling, and egg mixture.

Bake for 25 minutes, or until the tops are golden brown.

While the empanadas are baking, prepare the dipping sauce. Serve the empanadas hot or at room temperature with the sauce.

To roast garlic, start with a whole unpeeled head and cut just enough off the top to expose the ends of the individual cloves. Place on a square of foil, drizzle with about 3 tablespoons of extra-virgin olive oil, and wrap well to seal. Bake at 325°F for 45 to 60 minutes, until very soft. Let cool slightly, then squeeze the garlic from the skins.

CREAM CHEESE DOUGH

2 (8-ounce) packages cold cream cheese, cut into cubes
³⁄₄ pound (3 sticks) cold unsalted butter, cut into ¹⁄₂-inch slices
3 cups all-purpose flour
¹⁄₄ teaspoon sea salt

Place the cream cheese and butter in the bowl of a food processor. Add the flour and salt and pulse until just combined and starting to form a ball; do not overprocess. Gather the dough into a ball and divide in half. Flatten each piece into a disk and wrap with plastic wrap. Refrigerate for 1 hour.

BLACKBERRY CITRUS DIPPING SAUCE

I tablespoon unsalted butter
¹⁄₄ cup minced shallot
I¹⁄₄ cups fresh blackberries
¹⁄₄ cup raspberry vinegar
¹⁄₄ cup dry white wine
¹⁄₄ cup orange juice
2 tablespoons packed brown sugar
2 tablespoons maple syrup
2 tablespoons grated orange zest

Melt the butter in a medium saucepan over medium-high heat. Add the shallot and sauté for 1 minute. Add the blackberries, vinegar, wine, orange juice, brown sugar, maple syrup, and zest. Reduce the heat to medium and cook for 10 minutes.

Using a handheld blender or a food processor, blend until the blackberries are smooth. Strain into a bowl. Pour back into the saucepan and stir over high heat until the sauce is syrupy. Serve warm or at room temperature.

Gina's Grilled Lavender Avocados

Gina De Leone, a past employee of Mon Chéri Cooking School, developed this recipe many years ago, and it's been a favorite among students ever since. It's a whole new way to enjoy avocados. Serve with Lavender Margaritas (page 74) and a spoon to scoop out the warm, velvety flesh.

MAKES 6 SERVINGS

2 tablespoons unsalted butter,
    at room temperature
1 tablespoon fresh lime juice
1 tablespoon fresh lemon juice
1 tablespoon tequila
1/4 teaspoon dried culinary
    'Provence' lavender buds, finely
    ground in a spice grinder
1/8 teaspoon sea salt
3 avocados

Place the butter in a small bowl. Beat with a wooden spoon until thick and creamy. Add the lime juice, lemon juice, tequila, lavender, and salt. Beat until all the liquid is incorporated. Refrigerate until firm.

Preheat a grill to medium-high.

Halve the avocados, leaving the skin on but removing the pits. Place on the grill rack, flesh side down, and leave for 4 minutes to make grill marks on the avocados. Turn the avocados over and place 1 scant tablespoon of the butter mixture in the hollow of each half.

Grill for an additional 10 minutes, or until the butter melts and the avocado is soft. The cooking time depends on the ripeness of the avocado. The avocado should just bubble around the skin but not be overcooked.

Lavender Pecan Chicken Skewers
with Rhubarb-Apricot Dipping Sauce

The sweet-tart flavors of rhubarb and apricot go well with the lavender that's in both the sauce and the coating for the chicken. Pecans add unexpected crunch to the chicken. The sauce and the skewers are served at room temperature, so you can make them ahead.

MAKES 36 SKEWERS

6 boneless, skinless chicken breast
    halves, each cut into 6 long strips
1 cup all-purpose flour
2 large eggs
2 tablespoons water
1½ cups fresh bread crumbs
1 cup finely chopped pecans
1 tablespoon dried culinary
    'Provence' lavender buds, finely
    ground in a spice grinder
Sea salt and freshly ground
    black pepper
Rhubarb-Apricot Dipping Sauce
    (recipe follows)

Soak a package of 6-inch bamboo skewers in water for 30 minutes, then drain. Thread each chicken strip onto 2 skewers placed ¼ inch apart (the double skewers prevent the meat from twirling during grilling, making it easier to turn).

Place the flour in a shallow bowl. In a second shallow bowl, whisk together the eggs and water. In a third shallow bowl, mix the bread crumbs, pecans, and lavender; season with salt and pepper.

Dip the skewers into the flour to coat the chicken; shake off the excess. Dip into the eggs and then into the pecan mixture to coat thoroughly. Place in a single layer on 1 or 2 oiled baking sheets. Cover with plastic wrap and refrigerate for 1 hour.

While the skewers chill, prepare the dipping sauce.

Preheat the oven to 350°F. Bake the skewers for 15 minutes, or until the chicken is cooked through. Let cool. Serve at room temperature with the dipping sauce.

RHUBARB-APRICOT DIPPING SAUCE

1 cup sugar

1 cup water

½ pound fresh rhubarb, trimmed
and finely diced

½ cup golden raisins

¼ cup dried apricots, finely diced

¼ cup raspberry vinegar

2 tablespoons chopped onion

2 tablespoons chopped crystallized
ginger

1 tablespoon grated fresh ginger

1 tablespoon dried culinary
'Provence' lavender buds, finely
ground in a spice grinder

1 tablespoon dark molasses

1½ teaspoons Worcestershire sauce

½ teaspoon sea salt

½ teaspoon mustard seeds

¼ teaspoon hot-pepper sauce

1 garlic clove, minced

1 tablespoon grated lemon zest

½ cup crème fraîche (see note)

Bring the sugar and water to a simmer in a medium saucepan over medium heat and cook for 5 minutes. Add the rhubarb, raisins, apricots, vinegar, onion, crystallized ginger, fresh ginger, lavender, molasses, Worcestershire sauce, salt, mustard seeds, pepper sauce, and garlic. Simmer, stirring occasionally, for 20 minutes, or until thickened. Remove from the heat and stir in the lemon zest.

Let cool completely, then stir in the crème fraîche.

 Crème fraîche is a rich, thickened cream with a slightly tangy flavor. Look for it in upscale supermarkets or make your own, with or without lavender (see page 21).

BLUE CHEESE TORTA
WITH RASPBERRIES

Torta is Italian for "cake," and this blue cheese creation looks like a spectacular cake. Serve it with crackers and dried pears or dried peaches.

I prefer to use either a Maytag or a Saga blue cheese round because both are the right size and shape and have excellent flavor. You may use another creamy blue cheese if those are not available.

MAKES 30 SERVINGS

1 whole blue cheese wheel
    (about 5 pounds)
2 (8-ounce) packages cream
    cheese, at room temperature
½ pound (2 sticks) unsalted butter,
    at room temperature
2 tablespoons dried culinary
    'Provence' lavender buds, finely
    ground in a spice grinder
2 pints fresh raspberries
1 cup sugar
¼ cup water
1½ teaspoons unflavored gelatin
1 pint fresh raspberries

Cut the blue cheese horizontally into 3 even layers. Set aside the top and bottom layers. Crumble the middle layer into a large bowl. Beat with an electric mixer until smooth. Add the cream cheese, butter, and lavender. Beat until light and fluffy. Transfer the cheese mixture to a pastry bag fitted with a number 6 star tip.

In a food processor, blend 1½ cups of the raspberries until smooth. Strain through a fine-mesh sieve into a small bowl to remove the seeds. Stir in the sugar.

Place the water in a small saucepan and sprinkle with the gelatin. Let stand for 1 minute to soften. Stir over low heat for 1 to 2 minutes, or until the water is warm and the gelatin is dissolved. Stir in the raspberry puree and continue stirring to dissolve the sugar.

Place the bottom layer of the cheese wheel, cut side up, on a cardboard cake round or a decorative platter. Pipe large rosettes of the cream cheese mixture all around the top edge to make a solid border. Repeat to make a second layer of rosettes on top of the first (use about two-thirds of the mixture). Pour half of the raspberry puree in the center and top with about half of the remaining raspberries.

Replace the top cheese layer, cut side down, and coat with an even ½-inch layer of the cream cheese filling. Place a large leaf tip on the pastry bag and pipe a wreath of leaves around the edge. Fill the center with the remaining raspberry puree and decorate with the remaining raspberries.

Refrigerate for 2 hours, or until the gelatin in the raspberry puree sets.

Petite Lavender Scones

For me, nothing on earth is better than scones, clotted cream, and raspberry lavender jam. The basic scone is a treat that lends itself to all sorts of fruits and flavors, so it's no surprise that lavender enhances it immensely. Serve these scones with black lavender tea at any brunch or tea that you want to be truly memorable.

This recipe makes small scones. For larger ones, roll the dough 3/4 inch thick and use a 3-inch round cookie cutter. Increase the baking time to 18 minutes.

MAKES 65 SCONES

I tablespoon dried culinary
    'Provence' lavender buds
I cup plus 1/3 cup heavy cream
2 1/4 cups all-purpose flour
I tablespoon sugar
I teaspoon baking powder
1/4 teaspoon baking soda
1/4 pound (I stick) cold unsalted
    butter, cut into 1/4-inch slices
Lavender Sugar
    (page 19, optional)

Combine the lavender and I cup of the cream in a small saucepan. Bring to a boil over medium heat. Remove from the heat and let cool. Refrigerate for at least 2 hours. Strain the cream into a bowl and discard the lavender.

Preheat the oven to 375°F. Grease a baking sheet or line it with parchment paper.

In the bowl of a food processor, combine the flour, sugar, baking powder, and baking soda. Pulse to mix well. Scatter the butter over the flour. Pulse to make pea-size pieces. With the machine running, pour in the lavender cream. When mixture combines together to form a dough, stop the machine.

Place the dough on a lightly floured surface and roll to 1/2 inch thick. Using a 1 1/2-inch round cookie cutter, cut out as many rounds as possible. Reserve the dough scraps, combine into a ball, roll again, and cut more rounds. Only roll the scraps once.

Arrange the rounds I inch apart on the prepared baking sheet. Brush the tops with the remaining 1/3 cup cream for a glazed finish and sprinkle with lavender sugar (if using). Bake for 13 to 15 minutes, or until puffed and golden brown.

Lavender Thyme Mini-Muffins

Children love these muffins because they're "just my size." But you'll be equally enchanted with these savory, moist morsels that contain just a hint of lavender. Serve them piping hot with lots of butter.

MAKES 36 MUFFINS

Dough
2 tablespoons sugar
1 tablespoon dried culinary 'Provence' lavender buds, finely ground in a spice grinder
1 tablespoon minced shallot
2½ teaspoons (1 package) active dried yeast
1 teaspoon chopped chives
1 teaspoon fresh lemon thyme or thyme leaves
1 teaspoon sea salt
¼ teaspoon baking soda
2¼ cups all-purpose flour
¼ cup water
2 tablespoons unsalted butter
1 cup yogurt, at room temperature
1 large egg

Sesame Topping
1 large egg
1 tablespoon water
¼ teaspoon sea salt
1 tablespoon black sesame seeds
1 tablespoon white sesame seeds

To make the dough: In a large bowl, combine the sugar, lavender, shallot, yeast, chives, thyme, salt, baking soda, and ¼ cup of the flour. Beat with an electric mixer on low speed to combine.

Combine the water and butter in a small saucepan. Warm over low heat to about 130°F. Add to the bowl and beat until smooth, about 2 minutes. Add the yogurt, egg, and ½ cup of the remaining flour. Beat on high speed until smooth and elastic, about 2 minutes.

Add the remaining 1½ cups flour and beat again until smooth. Cover with plastic wrap and let rise in a warm place until doubled in size, about 45 minutes.

To make the topping: In a small bowl, combine the egg, water, and salt; beat with a fork until mixed well and thinned. In a cup, mix the black and white sesame seeds.

Preheat the oven to 350°F. Grease mini-muffin cups or coat with non-stick spray.

Using a wooden spoon, stir the batter 25 times. Spoon it into the prepared muffin cups. Brush the tops with the egg mixture and generously sprinkle with the sesame seeds.

Bake for 16 to 20 minutes, or until puffed and browned.

For uniform muffins every time, use a small, number 50 ice cream scoop to drop the dough into the prepared mini-muffin pans.

If you don't have enough muffin pans, bake the muffins in batches.

LAVENDER CRANBERRY SPARKLERS

Zesty lime and tart cranberry mingle with lavender to refresh and revitalize on warm spring days. Add a shot or two of vodka and you've got a perfect picnic drink. Serve in tall ice-filled glasses. Make two pitchers. It goes fast!

MAKES 8 SERVINGS

4 cups cranberry juice cocktail
¼ cup Lavender Syrup (page 20)
¼ cup sugar
3 tablespoons fresh lime juice
2 cups lime-flavored sparkling
    mineral water

In a pitcher, combine the juice, lavender syrup, sugar, and lime juice. Stir to dissolve the sugar. Add the mineral water just before serving.

Try this drink in martini glasses. Rub the rims with a lime and dip into Lavender Sugar (page 19).

LAVENDER ICED TEA SANGRIA

The secret to this refreshing, fruity iced tea is lavender black tea bags. Serve icy cold at afternoon parties and the cocktail hour.

MAKES 4 SERVINGS

4 cups water
4 lavender black tea bags (see note)
4 to 5 tablespoons sugar
1 peach or apple, peeled, pitted or
    seeded, and chopped
4 large strawberries, hulled and
    cut in half
1 orange, peeled and chopped
    into ¾-inch pieces
1 cup dry red wine

Bring the water to a boil in a medium saucepan. Remove from the heat and add the tea bags. Steep for 3 minutes, then remove the tea bags. Pour the tea into a pitcher and add the sugar. Stir until the sugar is dissolved. Cool. Can be made 1 day ahead. Cover and refrigerate.

In a bowl, mix the peach or apple, strawberries, and orange. Divide among four 16-ounce glasses and add ice. Add the wine to the pitcher and pour into the glasses.

Look for lavender black tea at fine tea and coffee houses. Murchie's makes an excellent one that you can order at www.murchies.com.

Asparagus Soup
with Lavender Lemon Cream

As spring arrives, so do tender new asparagus stalks. Make the most of this delicious spring vegetable with this fancy soup. Even without the lavender-scented lemon cream, you'll enjoy its herbal flavor. Serve with Lavender Thyme Mini-Muffins (page 32) or your favorite crostini.

MAKES 8 SERVINGS

3 pounds asparagus
2 tablespoons olive oil
1½ tablespoons unsalted butter
2 white onions, diced
2 medium russet potatoes, peeled
    and cubed
1 cup uncooked rice
6 cups chicken broth
1 tablespoon Glace de Poulet Gold
    (see note, optional)
¼ cup fresh Italian parsley leaves,
    chopped
1 teaspoon dried culinary
    'Provence' lavender buds, finely
    ground in a spice grinder
1 teaspoon dried thyme
¼ cup dry white wine
1 teaspoon grated lemon zest
¼ cup fresh lemon juice
1 teaspoon freshly ground white
    pepper
½ teaspoon sea salt
Lavender Lemon Cream
    (recipe follows)

Peel the asparagus and trim off the tough ends. Cut into 2-inch pieces, reserving the tips. Bring about 2 cups of water to a boil in a small saucepan. Add ½ cup of the asparagus tips and cook for 1 minute, until bright green and just barely tender. Drain and cover with cold water to stop the cooking. Drain and pat dry with paper towels; reserve for a garnish.

In a large stockpot over medium heat, warm the oil and butter until the butter melts. Add the onions and sauté until translucent, about 5 minutes. Stir in the potatoes and rice. Add the broth and glace de poulet (if using). Bring to a simmer and cook for 10 minutes.

Add the asparagus, parsley, lavender, and thyme. Simmer for 5 minutes, or until the potatoes and rice are tender. Using a handheld blender or a food processor (work in batches), blend the soup until smooth. If needed, return the soup to the pot. Add the wine, lemon zest, lemon juice, pepper, and salt. Bring to a gentle simmer and cook for 5 minutes.

Prepare the lemon cream.

To serve, pour the soup into individual bowls. Swirl each serving with 1 to 2 tablespoons of the lemon cream (or place the lemon cream in a squeeze bottle and drizzle over the soup in a decorative pattern). Top with the reserved asparagus tips. Serve immediately.

Glace de Poulet Gold is a chicken-stock concentrate. It enriches the flavor of regular broth or stock. You can find this product at most upscale supermarkets and specialty food stores or at www.morethangourmet.com.

Lavender Lemon Cream

½ cup crème fraîche (see note)

¼ teaspoon very finely grated
    lemon zest

2 tablespoons fresh lemon juice

½ teaspoon dried culinary
    'Provence' lavender buds, finely
    ground in a spice grinder

In a small bowl, mix the crème fraîche, lemon zest, lemon juice, and lavender.

 Crème fraîche is a rich, thickened cream with a slightly tangy flavor. Look for it in upscale supermarkets or make your own, with or without lavender (see page 21).

Lavender Tropical Fruit Gazpacho

Something pretty in pink and sweet to eat! Serve this refreshing, fruity gazpacho at the beginning of a romantic dinner for two or a special dinner for friends. If you want to serve this for Valentine's Day and fresh berries are not available, you may use unsweetened frozen berries.

Both the lavender syrup and the pureed fruit can be prepared a day ahead and refrigerated, but the fresh fruit tastes best if you eat it the same day.

MAKES 6 SERVINGS

1½ cups water

½ cup sugar

1 teaspoon dried culinary
    'Provence' lavender buds, finely
    ground in a spice grinder

1 pint fresh raspberries

1 mango, peeled, seeded, and cut
    into chunks

1 papaya, peeled, seeded, and diced

¼ cup fresh lime juice

2 pints fresh strawberries, hulled

¼ cup unsweetened coconut milk

1 kiwifruit, peeled and diced

6 pineapple wedges (garnish)

Fresh mint sprigs (garnish)

In a medium saucepan, combine the water, sugar, and lavender. Simmer over medium heat for 3 minutes, or until the sugar is completely dissolved. Refrigerate for 1 hour, or until cold. Strain out the lavender.

In a blender or food processor, combine the raspberries, mango, papaya, lime juice, and 1 pint of the strawberries. Blend until smooth. Pour into a large glass or stainless steel bowl. Dice the remaining 1 pint strawberries and add to the bowl. Stir in the cold sugar syrup, coconut milk, and kiwifruit. Cover and refrigerate for at least 2 hours.

To serve, ladle into chilled martini or margarita glasses. Cut a slit in each pineapple wedge so you can slide it onto the side of the glass. Garnish with fresh mint sprigs. Serve immediately.

Fruitful Salad with Lavender Candied Pecans
and Pomegranate Dressing

The sweet-sour dressing pairs well with the bitter greens. This dish can be a light meal in itself by adding diced grilled chicken (try the Grilled Lavender Honey Breast of Chicken on page 86).

MAKES 6 TO 8 SERVINGS

Lavender Candied Pecans
(recipe follows)
Pomegranate Dressing
(recipe follows)
4 cups loosely packed baby spinach,
rinsed and dried
1 small head butter lettuce,
washed, dried, and torn into
bite-size pieces
2 small heads radicchio, outer
leaves discarded and the rest
shredded
2 avocados, halved, pitted, peeled,
and cut into small wedges
2 mangoes, peeled, pitted, and
thinly sliced
2 cups seedless red grapes,
cut in half
2 tart green apples, cored and
thinly sliced

Prepare the pecans.

Prepare the dressing.

In a large bowl, toss together the spinach, lettuce, and radicchio. Add half of the dressing and toss to coat. Mound onto a large serving platter.

In the same bowl, combine the avocados, mangoes, grapes, and apples. Add the remaining dressing and toss gently to coat. Spoon over the greens. Sprinkle with the pecans and serve immediately.

Lavender Candied Pecans

¾ cup pecan halves or large pieces
2 tablespoons Lavender Sugar
(page 19)
1 teaspoon unsalted butter

Butter a baking sheet and set aside. Place the pecans in a large skillet and stir over high heat for about 4 minutes, or until lightly browned and fragrant. Add the sugar and reduce the heat to medium. Cook, stirring constantly, until the sugar is melted and just beginning to caramelize.

Stir in the butter and immediately transfer the nuts to the prepared baking sheet. Cool completely, then break up any nut clusters.

POMEGRANATE DRESSING

½ cup extra-virgin olive oil

¼ cup mango nectar

2 tablespoons Ruby Red grapefruit
juice

2 tablespoons pomegranate
molasses (see note)

1 teaspoon balsamic vinegar

1 teaspoon dried culinary
'Provence' lavender buds, finely
ground in a spice grinder

Sea salt and freshly ground black
pepper

In a small bowl, whisk together the oil, mango nectar, grapefruit juice, molasses, vinegar, and lavender. Season with salt and pepper.

Pomegranate molasses is available at most international and Middle Eastern food markets. You can also order it at www.deandeluca.com.

Farro Lavender Tabbouleh Salad

Farro is an ancient Italian grain that's enjoying a resurgence of popularity. It looks like light brown rice and has a nutty taste. Here, it takes the place of the more commonly used bulgur wheat. The addition of garbanzo beans makes this protein-rich salad an excellent choice for vegetarian guests.

Soaking farro overnight plumps the grain, giving it a superior texture and maximizing the flavor. Soaking also reduces the cooking time from 45 minutes to a quick 5 to 10 minutes.

MAKES 10 TO 12 SERVINGS

4 cups water
1½ cups uncooked farro (12 ounces)
Sea salt
Citrus Vinaigrette (recipe follows)
1 cup canned garbanzo beans,
    rinsed and drained
4 Roma (Italian) tomatoes,
    seeded and diced
2 large green onions, thinly sliced
1 large red onion, diced
1 carrot, diced
1 small zucchini, diced
1 small yellow squash, diced
½ cup diced red bell pepper
1 cup fresh Italian parsley leaves,
    chopped
1 tablespoon fresh mint leaves,
    chopped
1 teaspoon dried culinary
    'Provence' lavender buds, finely
    ground in a spice grinder
1 garlic clove, minced
Freshly ground black pepper

Place the water and farro in a large bowl. Let soak for 8 hours, or overnight.

Drain the farro and transfer to a large stockpot. Cover with 2 inches of cold water and add 1 tablespoon of the salt. Bring to a boil over high heat and cook for 5 to 10 minutes, or until the farro is just tender to the bite. Drain in a colander, shaking off the excess water.

Prepare the vinaigrette.

Transfer the farro to a bowl and stir in ½ cup of the vinaigrette. Spread the farro in an even layer on a rimmed baking sheet and refrigerate until cool.

In a large bowl, combine the beans, tomatoes, green onions, red onion, carrot, zucchini, yellow squash, bell pepper, parsley, mint, lavender, and garlic. Add the remaining vinaigrette and toss well. Add the farro and toss well. Season with salt and pepper.

Citrus Vinaigrette

1 cup extra-virgin olive oil
½ cup orange juice
¼ cup fresh lemon juice
¼ cup sherry vinegar or lavender
    vinegar
3 tablespoons honey
2 teaspoons grated orange zest
Sea salt and freshly ground black
    pepper

In a blender, combine the oil, orange juice, lemon juice, vinegar, honey, and orange zest; blend until creamy and smooth. (Or combine the ingredients in a bowl and use a handheld blender to emulsify them.) Season with salt and pepper.

GRILLED MEDITERRANEAN LAMB SALAD
WITH LAVENDER ARTICHOKES

Lamb is often considered a dish reserved for company, but you needn't save it just for special occasions. This salad is a good choice for casual dinners. It's bountiful and is a meal in itself when served with a crusty loaf of olive bread.

MAKES 8 SERVINGS

Lavender Artichokes
(recipe follows)
Warm Grilled Lamb
(recipe follows)
Sun-Dried Tomato Vinaigrette
(recipe follows)
1 head romaine lettuce
4 cups assorted mixed spring greens
1 pound asparagus, peeled, trimmed, and steamed
6 small portobello mushrooms, sliced
3/4 cup cherry tomatoes, cut in half
1 red bell pepper, thinly sliced

Prepare the artichokes.

Prepare the lamb.

Prepare the vinaigrette.

Place a romaine lettuce leaf on each dinner plate. Mound the spring greens equally on the leaves. Fan out pieces of the warm lamb on top of the leaves. Arrange the artichokes, asparagus, mushrooms, tomatoes, and pepper around the lamb in a decorative circular pattern. Drizzle the vinaigrette over the salads. Serve immediately.

LAVENDER ARTICHOKES

4 cups water
1 cup dry white wine
1/2 medium onion, sliced
2 tablespoons sherry vinegar or red wine vinegar
1 teaspoon dried thyme, crumbled
1 teaspoon dried culinary 'Provence' lavender buds, finely ground in a spice grinder
10 whole black peppercorns
4 large artichokes, cut in half lengthwise

In a large pot, combine the water, wine, onion, vinegar, thyme, lavender, and peppercorns. Bring to a boil over medium-high heat. Add the artichokes, cut side down. Cover and reduce the heat. Simmer, turning once, for 40 minutes, or until the artichokes are tender when pierced with a sharp knife. Transfer the artichokes to a bowl using a slotted spoon. Discard the cooking liquid.

Warm Grilled Lamb

¼ pound (1 stick) unsalted butter,
   at room temperature
¼ cup Dijon mustard
2 shallots, minced
2 tablespoons fresh Italian parsley
   leaves, chopped
2 tablespoons chopped chives
1 tablespoon dried culinary
   'Provence' lavender buds, finely
   ground in a spice grinder
4 to 6 fresh rosemary sprigs,
   woody stems removed and leaves
   finely chopped
6 garlic cloves, finely chopped
Freshly ground black pepper
1 (3-pound) lamb loin, boned,
   rolled, and tied

Preheat a grill to medium-high.

In a small bowl, mix the butter, mustard, shallots, parsley, chives, lavender, rosemary, and garlic. Season with pepper. Place the lamb on the hot grill and cook, brushing frequently with the herb butter, for 30 to 35 minutes, or until the internal temperature reaches 125° to 135°F on an instant-read thermometer. The lamb should be light pink. Discard any remaining butter. Cut the lamb into paper-thin slices.

Sun-Dried Tomato Vinaigrette

⅔ cup extra-virgin olive oil
⅔ cup fresh lemon juice
⅓ cup champagne vinegar
3 tablespoons Dijon mustard
3 garlic cloves, cut in half
1 teaspoon sea salt
¼ teaspoon freshly ground black
   pepper
1 bunch fresh basil
¼ cup oil-packed sun-dried
   tomatoes, blotted of excess oil
   and julienned

In a blender, combine the oil, lemon juice, vinegar, mustard, garlic, salt, and pepper. Tear the basil leaves from their stems and add to the blender. Blend until smooth and creamy. Pour into a bowl and stir in the tomatoes. Refrigerate until needed.

Grilled Lavender Halibut in Banana Leaves
with Tropical Raspberry Salsa

Your guests will be delighted when they open these banana-leaf packets. The scent of citrus, Kaffir lime leaves, and lavender will fill the room. A fragrant fruit salsa makes a flawless accompaniment to this dramatic entrée. Serve with Hawaiian Macadamia Lavender Rice (page 53).

Look for banana leaves and Kaffir lime leaves at Asian markets. Also try asking your local Thai restaurant if you can buy some of their leaves. Be aware that banana leaves are inedible. Wasabi powder, that fiery green Japanese horseradish, can be found in the Asian food section of most supermarkets.

MAKES 4 SERVINGS

**Citrus Lavender Herb Butter
(recipe follows)**
**Raspberry, Mango, and Papaya
Salsa (recipe follows)**
**1 (1-pound) package frozen
banana leaves, thawed and
soaked in water**
**4 (6-ounce) halibut fillets, 1¼
to 1½ inches thick, skin and
bones removed**
**Sea salt and freshly ground black
pepper**
4 Kaffir lime leaves (optional)
1 lemon, cut into thin slices
1 lime, cut into thin slices
**1 tablespoon dried culinary
'Provence' lavender buds, finely
ground in a spice grinder**

Preheat a grill to medium.

Prepare the herb butter.

Prepare the salsa.

Cut the banana leaves into eight equal sheets large enough to wrap around the fillets. For each packet, overlap two banana leaves to form a cross. Place a fish fillet in the center of each cross and season both sides with salt and pepper. Spread 1 slightly rounded tablespoon of the herb butter on top of each fillet.

Top each fillet with 1 lime leaf (if using), 1 lemon slice, and 1 lime slice. Sprinkle evenly with the lavender. Tie each package with a 24-inch piece of kitchen string, covering both directions.

Grill over indirect heat, turning once, for 7 to 8 minutes per side (14 to 16 minutes total). Cut the string and transfer the packets to a platter lined with additional banana leaves. Serve with the salsa on the side. Guests can open their own packets after being served.

Citrus Lavender Herb Butter

6 ounces (1½ sticks) unsalted butter
1 tablespoon grated lime zest
1 tablespoon grated lemon zest
¼ cup fresh lime juice
¼ cup fresh lemon juice
1½ tablespoons lavender vinegar
    or raspberry vinegar
1 tablespoon honey mustard
½ teaspoon wasabi powder
¼ cup fresh cilantro leaves, chopped
¼ cup minced chives
2 shallots, minced
1 tablespoon grated fresh ginger
    (see note)
1 tablespoon minced garlic

In a food processor, combine the butter, lime zest, lemon zest, lime juice, lemon juice, vinegar, mustard, and wasabi. Blend until smooth. Add the cilantro, chives, shallots, ginger, and garlic. Blend until mixed well.

It's best to peel ginger before grating it. The easiest way to scrape away the thin skin is with a small serving spoon. Then use a ginger grater or the smallest holes on a regular grater to grate the root finely.

Raspberry, Mango, and Papaya Salsa

1 cup peeled and diced Asian pear
1 tablespoon grated lime zest
3 tablespoons fresh lime juice
1 tablespoon dried culinary
    'Provence' lavender buds, finely
    ground in a spice grinder
1 large mango, peeled, pitted,
    and diced
1 cup peeled, seeded, and diced
    papaya
2 tablespoons finely chopped
    crystallized ginger
2 teaspoons thinly sliced (on the
    diagonal) green onion
2 cups fresh raspberries

In a medium bowl, mix the pear, lime zest, lime juice, and lavender. Add the mango, papaya, ginger, and green onion; toss to mix well. Toss in the raspberries just before serving.

Lavender Chicken Breasts

in Champagne Sauce

We call this "Romancing the Kitchen"! Share glasses of Champagne while you and your sweetheart prepare this lavender-perfumed dish. It's so quick and easy that you'll be enjoying your candlelit dinner in no time!

For dessert, make a batch of Chocolate Lavender Brownies (page 55) ahead of time. Add your favorite decadent ice cream and you'll be well on your way to an enchanted evening.

MAKES 6 SERVINGS

6 boneless, skinless chicken breast halves

¼ cup fresh lemon juice

1 teaspoon dried thyme

1 teaspoon dried culinary 'Provence' lavender buds, finely ground in a spice grinder

Sea salt and freshly ground black pepper

1 tablespoon extra-virgin olive oil

4 tablespoons plus 1 teaspoon unsalted butter, at room temperature

2 cups thinly sliced small brown mushrooms

½ cup minced shallot

½ cup Champagne

½ cup chicken broth

1 tablespoon Glace de Poulet Gold (see note, optional)

1 teaspoon all-purpose flour

2 tablespoons fresh Italian parsley leaves, finely chopped

Fresh thyme sprigs or lavender sprigs (garnish)

Sprinkle both sides of the chicken with the lemon juice, thyme, and lavender. Let marinate for 20 minutes. Season lightly with salt and pepper.

Place the oil and 4 tablespoons of the butter in a large skillet and set over medium-high heat until the butter melts. Add the chicken and brown on both sides, about 7 minutes. Remove the chicken from the skillet and set aside.

Add the mushrooms and shallot to the skillet. Sauté for 4 to 5 minutes, stirring constantly. Add the Champagne, broth, and glace de poulet (if using). Simmer for 10 minutes.

In a cup, mix the flour and the remaining 1 teaspoon butter. Whisk into the skillet and continue whisking until the sauce thickens, about 2 minutes. Return the chicken to the skillet and simmer for 15 minutes. Add the parsley and transfer to a platter. Garnish with the thyme or lavender sprigs.

Glace de Poulet Gold is a chicken-stock concentrate. It enriches the flavor of regular broth or stock. You can find this product at most upscale supermarkets and specialty food stores or at www.morethangourmet.com.

CONFETTI CRAB AND BLACK BEAN ROULADE
with RED PEPPER AND TOMATO COULIS

This beautiful roulade turns any brunch into a special occasion. Accompany the roulade with Lavender Tropical Fruit Gazpacho (page 35) and Lavender Tangerine Mimosas (page 75).

Be sure to prepare the coulis recipe before starting the roulade since you will need the oven for both. You'll also need some roasted peppers from the coulis to put in the roulade.

MAKES 6 TO 8 SERVINGS

Red Pepper and Tomato Coulis (recipe follows)
2 tablespoons unsalted butter
½ cup minced green onion
¼ cup finely diced roasted red bell pepper (from coulis recipe)
¼ cup finely diced roasted yellow bell pepper (from coulis recipe)
1 tablespoon dried culinary 'Provence' lavender buds, finely ground in a spice grinder
1 cup fresh crabmeat
1 cup rinsed and drained canned black beans
1 tablespoon fresh lemon juice
¼ cup (2 ounces) cream cheese, at room temperature
2 cups heavy cream
6 large eggs
½ teaspoon sea salt
1 bunch chives, finely chopped (garnish)

Preheat the broiler and prepare the tomato coulis.

Reset the oven temperature to 325°F. Grease a 15 x 10-inch jelly-roll pan and line with a sheet of parchment paper.

Melt the butter in a large skillet over medium heat. Add the green onion, red pepper, yellow pepper, and lavender. Sauté for 5 minutes, or until translucent. Remove from the heat.

Pick through the crabmeat to remove any pieces of shell or cartilage. Stir the crabmeat, beans, and lemon juice into the skillet.

Place the cream cheese in a large bowl and beat with an electric mixer until smooth. Slowly beat in the cream to mix well. Beat in the eggs and salt. Fold in the crab mixture. Pour into the prepared jelly-roll pan and smooth the top.

Bake for 30 minutes, or until the top is golden brown and springs back when touched lightly. Remove from the oven and let cool on a wire rack for 5 minutes.

Loosen the edges of the roll with a spatula. Cover with a clean piece of parchment paper and a baking sheet. Invert. Remove the jelly-roll pan and peel off the parchment paper.

Starting at a long edge, tightly roll the egg mixture into a log. Place on a serving platter. Garnish with chopped chives. Serve immediately, accompanied by the coulis.

Red Pepper and Tomato Coulis

4 extra-large red bell peppers
1 yellow bell pepper
Grated zest from 1 lemon
Sea salt and freshly ground black
   pepper
Pinch of sugar (optional)
3 very ripe red tomatoes, peeled,
   seeded, and finely diced

Preheat the broiler. Place the peppers on a baking sheet and broil about 4 inches from the heat until blackened on top. Turn with tongs and continue broiling until blackened on all sides. Set aside until cool enough to handle. Remove the blackened skin and the inner seeds and membranes.

Finely dice $1/4$ cup of red pepper and set aside for the roulade. Finely dice $1/4$ cup of yellow pepper and set aside for the roulade; reserve the remainder of the yellow pepper for another use.

Place the remaining red peppers in a food processor. Add the lemon zest and season with salt and pepper. Blend until smooth. Transfer to a saucepan. If the sauce is bitter, add a pinch of sugar. Warm over medium heat. If the sauce is too thin, simmer for a few minutes until thickened. Stir in the tomatoes. Serve warm.

Lavender Chicken with Avocado Cream Sauce
on a Bed of Linguine

Serve this at parties and your guests won't stop talking about it. Basic pasta and chicken are greatly enhanced by unexpected ingredients: Cognac, avocados, Gorgonzola, pistachios, and—of course—lavender.

MAKES 4 TO 6 SERVINGS

1 pound dry linguine pasta

6 tablespoons unsalted butter

1½ pounds boneless, skinless chicken breasts

Sea salt and freshly ground black pepper

¼ pound cremini mushrooms, quartered

1 tablespoon minced shallot

1 tablespoon dried culinary 'Provence' lavender buds, finely ground in a spice grinder

1 cup heavy cream

⅓ cup chicken broth

2 tablespoons Cognac or brandy

2 ripe avocados

2 tablespoons fresh lemon juice

1 cup crumbled Gorgonzola or Cambozola cheese

⅓ cup unsalted pistachio nuts, toasted and coarsely chopped (garnish)

2 tablespoons fresh Italian parsley leaves, finely chopped (garnish)

Bring 3 quarts of water to a boil in a large pot. Add the pasta and cook for 10 minutes, or until just tender to the bite. Drain well, return the pasta to the pot, and set over low heat. Add 4 tablespoons of the butter and stir until the butter melts and coats the strands (this prevents the pasta from sticking).

While the pasta water boils, cut each chicken breast into 6 or 7 strips. Sprinkle with salt and pepper.

Melt the remaining 2 tablespoons butter in a large skillet over high heat until hot but not browned. Add the chicken. Cook, stirring often, for 3 to 4 minutes, or until the chicken is just cooked through. Remove the chicken with a slotted spoon and set aside.

Add the mushrooms, shallot, and lavender to the skillet. Stir for 3 minutes. In a small bowl, mix the cream, broth, and Cognac or brandy. Stir into the skillet. Cook for 5 minutes, or until thickened. Season with salt and pepper. Reduce the heat to medium-low, stir in the chicken, and heat through.

Halve, pit, and peel the avocados. Dice 1 avocado and stir into the skillet.

Slice the other avocado into ½-inch wedges and place in a medium bowl. Add the lemon juice and toss to coat.

Transfer the pasta to a serving platter and top with the chicken mixture. Sprinkle with the cheese. Garnish with the pistachios, parsley, and avocado wedges.

Spicy Steak Salad
with Lavender Caesar Dressing

Lavender goes well with red meat. Here, it harmonizes perfectly with other spices to make a tantalizing rub. This substantial salad, with its piquant dressing, is a crowd pleaser for al fresco dining.

MAKES 8 TO 10 SERVINGS

Spicy Marinated Steak
    (recipe follows)
Lavender Caesar Dressing
    (recipe follows)
2 large heads romaine lettuce,
    torn into bite-size pieces
1 (14½-ounce) can black beans,
    rinsed and drained
½ cup fresh cilantro leaves
¼ cup sliced green onion
2 cups assorted pear-shaped
    tomatoes, cut in half
2 cups corn chips, coarsely
    crumbled
4 or 5 medium avocados, halved,
    pitted, peeled, and cut into
    ¼-inch slices
Sour cream (garnish)

Prepare the steak.

Prepare the dressing.

In a large bowl, toss together the lettuce, beans, cilantro, and green onion. Pour on 1 cup of the dressing and toss to coat. Transfer to a large platter, making a bed of lettuce in the middle. Place the sliced beef around the edge of the lettuce. Put the tomatoes next to the meat and the corn chips in the very center of the salad. Top with the avocados. Garnish with sour cream and serve with the remaining dressing on the side.

Spicy Marinated Steak

¾ cup dry white wine
¼ cup extra-virgin olive oil
¼ cup lavender honey
¼ cup Dijon mustard
¼ cup grated lemon zest
1½ teaspoons fresh lemon juice
1 tablespoon cracked black
   peppercorns
1 tablespoon dried culinary
   'Provence' lavender buds, finely
   ground in a spice grinder
¼ teaspoon sea salt
2 pounds flank steak

In a medium bowl, mix the wine, oil, honey, mustard, lemon zest, lemon juice, pepper, lavender, and salt. Rub over the steak on all sides. Place on a plate, cover, and refrigerate for 6 hours or overnight.

Preheat a grill to medium. Grill the steak to the desired doneness (about 5 minutes per side for medium). Let stand for 10 minutes before slicing across the grain and on the diagonal.

Lavender Caesar Dressing

2 cups ricotta cheese
½ cup extra-virgin olive oil
½ cup country-style Dijon mustard
⅓ cup grated Parmesan cheese
¼ cup fresh lime juice
¼ cup fresh cilantro leaves,
   chopped
1 tablespoon minced garlic
2 teaspoons anchovy paste
2 teaspoons ground coriander
2 teaspoons dried culinary
   'Provence' lavender buds, finely
   ground in a spice grinder
1½ teaspoons crushed hot-pepper
   flakes
1 teaspoon ground cumin
½ teaspoon chili powder

In a blender, combine the ricotta, oil, mustard, Parmesan, lime juice, cilantro, garlic, anchovy paste, coriander, lavender, pepper flakes, cumin, and chili powder. Blend until smooth and creamy. Pour into a bowl, cover, and refrigerate until needed.

Sautéed Cremini Mushrooms
with Baby Onions and Lavender

These lavender-scented mushrooms are an excellent accompaniment to a good steak, grilled chicken, or mixed grill. In fact, they're great for any cookout. For best results, use mushrooms that are less than an inch across.

MAKES 6 SERVINGS

4 tablespoons unsalted butter

¼ cup extra-virgin olive oil

2 (10-ounce) packages frozen pearl onions, thawed

1½ pounds small cremini mushrooms (see note)

½ cup lavender vinegar or sherry vinegar

⅓ cup oil-packed sun-dried tomatoes, blotted of excess oil and julienned

9 ounces smoked mozzarella, cut into ½-inch cubes

1 teaspoon dried culinary 'Provence' lavender buds, finely ground in a spice grinder

Sea salt and freshly ground black pepper

2 or 3 fresh lavender sprigs (garnish)

Heat the butter and oil in a large skillet over medium heat. Add the onions and sauté for 10 to 15 minutes, or until lightly caramelized.

Increase the heat to medium-high, add the mushrooms, and sauté until they release their liquid. Continue cooking until all the liquid evaporates. Add the vinegar and tomatoes and simmer for 3 minutes, or until the liquid thickens slightly. Transfer to a large bowl.

Add the mozzarella to the bowl and toss to combine. Add the lavender and season with salt and pepper. Transfer to a serving platter and garnish with the lavender sprigs.

Wipe mushrooms clean with paper towels or a mushroom brush. Generally, it's best not to wash mushrooms. They begin to turn brown when you wash them. And they absorb water, which dilutes their flavor.

For this dish, if your mushrooms are especially dirty or if you're in a hurry, you *could* rinse them in a colander under cold running water just before using. Dry them in a salad spinner or on paper towels. Cooking them right after rinsing prevents discoloration, while sautéing evaporates any absorbed water.

Asparagus with Lavender, Pine Nuts, and Mozzarella Balls

Make this when lovely spring asparagus is abundant. Lemon brings out the flavor of the asparagus, and the pine nuts add elegance to this simple side dish. Bocconcini are small mozzarella balls, about an inch in diameter.

MAKES 6 SERVINGS

2 pounds pencil-thin asparagus

$\frac{1}{4}$ cup extra-virgin olive oil

$\frac{1}{4}$ teaspoon crushed hot-pepper flakes

2 garlic cloves, minced

$\frac{1}{2}$ cup pine nuts

1 teaspoon dried culinary 'Provence' lavender buds, finely ground in a spice grinder

$\frac{1}{2}$ teaspoon sea salt

$\frac{1}{8}$ teaspoon freshly ground black pepper

$\frac{1}{2}$ pound fresh bocconcini mozzarella balls, quartered

1 tablespoon grated lemon zest

1 tablespoon fresh lemon juice

Peel the asparagus stalks and trim off the tough ends. Cook in boiling salted water for 3 minutes. Drain and cover with cold water to stop the cooking. Drain and pat dry with paper towels.

Warm the olive oil in a large skillet over medium heat. Add the pepper flakes and garlic; stir for 1 minute. Add the pine nuts; sauté for a few minutes, until the nuts just begin to color. Add the asparagus and lavender; sauté for about 3 minutes, until just heated through. Season with the salt and pepper.

Transfer to a platter and top with the mozzarella; allow the heat from the asparagus to melt the cheese slightly. Sprinkle with the lemon zest and drizzle with the lemon juice.

LAVENDER LEMON BUTTERED CARROTS

If you think carrots aren't very interesting, this easy recipe will change your mind. It goes particularly well with Lavender Chicken Breasts in Champagne Sauce (page 44).

(page 44)

MAKES 6 SERVINGS

2 pounds medium carrots
   (about 4 or 5)
1 cup water
1½ teaspoons dried culinary
   'Provence' lavender buds, finely
   ground in a spice grinder
1 lemon
3 tablespoons unsalted butter
2 tablespoons extra-virgin olive oil
1 garlic clove, minced
½ teaspoon fresh lemon thyme or
   thyme leaves
2 tablespoons fresh Italian parsley
   leaves, chopped
½ teaspoon sea salt
⅛ teaspoon freshly ground white
   pepper

Cut the carrots on the diagonal into ½-inch slices. Place in a medium saucepan with the water and lavender. Cover and cook over medium heat for 15 minutes, or until fork tender. Drain all but 1 tablespoon of liquid.

Grate the zest off the lemon. Cut the lemon in half and squeeze the juice from one half into a cup. Cut the remaining half into thin slices.

Heat the butter and oil in a large skillet over medium heat. Add the garlic and sauté for 1 minute, until soft but not brown. Add the carrots, the reserved liquid, thyme, lemon zest, lemon juice, and 1 tablespoon of the parsley. Cover and cook over low heat for 1 minute. Season with the salt and pepper. Decoratively arrange the lemon slices over the carrots and sprinkle with the remaining parsley.

Hawaiian Macadamia Lavender Rice

This aromatic rice dish gets added texture from the chopped macadamia nuts. Serve with Grilled Lavender Halibut in Banana Leaves with Tropical Raspberry Salsa (page 42) or other exotically flavored main courses.

MAKES 6 TO 8 SERVINGS

1 cup finely chopped onion
2 tablespoons extra-virgin olive oil
1 tablespoon grated fresh ginger
1 garlic clove, minced
1 cup uncooked basmati rice
2½ cups chicken broth
½ teaspoon sea salt
1 cup coarsely chopped macadamia
    nuts
1 tablespoon grated lemon zest
2 tablespoons unsalted butter
1 teaspoon dried culinary
    'Provence' lavender buds, finely
    ground in a spice grinder
Freshly ground black pepper

In a medium saucepan, combine the onion, oil, ginger, and garlic. Stir over medium heat for 5 minutes, or until soft. Stir in the rice and then the broth and salt. Bring to a simmer. Cover, reduce the heat to medium-low, and cook for 20 minutes, or until the rice is tender and all the liquid has been absorbed.

Remove from the heat. Stir in the nuts and lemon zest. Cover and let stand for 5 minutes. Gently stir in the butter and lavender. Season with pepper.

LAVENDER APPLE RHUBARB CRISP

Make this lovely crisp when ruby-red stalks of rhubarb appear in supermarkets in the spring. This sweet-tart dessert is especially good served with vanilla ice cream or a big dollop of sweetened whipped cream to which you've added a little ground lavender.

MAKES 6 SERVINGS

Topping
½ cup pecan halves or large pieces
1 cup all-purpose flour
½ cup sugar
¼ teaspoon salt
¼ pound (1 stick) cold unsalted
    butter, cut into ½-inch slices

Fruit
4 large Granny Smith apples
3 tablespoons fresh lemon juice
2 teaspoons vanilla extract
4 or 5 large rhubarb stalks
2 tablespoons dried culinary
    'Provence' lavender buds
¾ cup sugar
3 tablespoons all-purpose flour
2 teaspoons ground cinnamon

Preheat the oven to 350°F. Butter a 13 x 9-inch baking dish.

To make the topping: Place the pecans in a food processor and pulse until coarsely chopped. Transfer to a cup and set aside. Place the flour, sugar, and salt in the food processor. Scatter the butter on top. Pulse until the mixture resembles coarse crumbs.

To make the fruit: Peel and core the apples; cut into ½-inch slices (you should have about 6 cups). Place in a large bowl and toss with the lemon juice and vanilla. Cut the rhubarb into ¼-inch slices (you should have about 4 cups). Add to the bowl.

Place the lavender in a spice grinder with ¼ cup of the sugar. Pulse until the lavender is finely ground. Transfer to a small bowl. Stir in the flour, cinnamon, and the remaining ½ cup sugar. Sprinkle over the fruit and toss to combine.

Transfer the fruit mixture to the prepared baking dish. Sprinkle with the pecans. Sprinkle with the crumb mixture. Bake for 50 to 60 minutes, or until the fruit is bubbling and the topping is golden brown. Serve warm.

Placing the chopped nuts under the crumb mixture helps keep the nuts from burning.

CHOCOLATE LAVENDER BROWNIES

I love these brownies! They're moist, chewy, and so quick and easy to prepare. Why bother making brownies from a box, when these take only a few extra minutes and taste so much better? Serve them with vanilla ice cream topped with hot fudge sauce—or just plain with a glass of cold milk. What could be better?

MAKES 24 BROWNIES

1 teaspoon dried culinary
    'Provence' lavender buds

3 cups sugar

1³⁄₄ cups all-purpose flour

³⁄₄ cup plus 2 tablespoons
    unsweetened Dutch-process
    cocoa powder (see note)

¹⁄₂ teaspoon salt

¹⁄₄ teaspoon instant espresso powder
    or instant coffee powder

³⁄₄ pound (3 sticks) unsalted butter

4 large eggs

2 teaspoons vanilla extract

1 cup chopped walnuts or pecans
    (optional)

Preheat the oven to 325°F. Butter a 13 x 9-inch baking dish.

Place the lavender in a spice grinder with 1 tablespoon of the sugar. Pulse until the lavender is finely ground. Transfer to a large bowl. Add the flour, cocoa, salt, espresso or coffee powder, and the remaining sugar. Mix well.

Place the butter in a medium microwave-safe bowl and microwave on high power for 1 minute at a time until melted. Let cool for a few minutes. Whisk in the eggs and vanilla.

Make a well in the center of the dry ingredients and pour in the butter mixture. Using a wooden spoon, mix until just combined. Stir in the nuts (if using). Pour into the prepared pan and smooth the top. Bake for 35 to 45 minutes, until a toothpick inserted in the center comes out mostly clean.

Dutch-process cocoa has been treated with an alkali to neutralize cocoa's natural acidity. It tends to be darker and richer than regular cocoa. Look for it in the baking aisle with other cocoa powder.

Lemon Ginger Cupcakes
with Lavender Cream Cheese Frosting

Cupcakes as bright as the sunshine! What could be more cheerful at a spring picnic? Serve with Lavender Ginger Lemonade (page 73) to make this an extra-special treat.

This batter makes a lot of cupcakes. Just use your regular muffin pan and bake the cupcakes in batches.

MAKES 34 CUPCAKES

3 cups cake flour
2 teaspoons ground ginger
1 teaspoon baking powder
1 teaspoon baking soda
½ teaspoon salt
2 cups sugar
6 ounces (1½ sticks) unsalted
    butter, at room temperature
4 large eggs
1 teaspoon grated orange zest
1 teaspoon grated lemon zest
3 tablespoons fresh lemon juice
2 tablespoons dried culinary
    'Provence' lavender buds, finely
    ground in a spice grinder
1 teaspoon vanilla extract
1¼ cups buttermilk
¼ cup finely chopped crystallized
    ginger
2 tablespoons poppy seeds
Lavender Cream Cheese Frosting
    (recipe follows)
¼ cup large-crystal, lavender-
    colored sparkling sugar
    (see note)

Preheat the oven to 350°F. Line 12 muffin cups with paper liners.

Sift the flour, ground ginger, baking powder, baking soda, and salt into a medium bowl or onto a sheet of wax paper.

Combine the sugar and butter in a large bowl. Beat with an electric mixer until smooth. Add 1 egg at a time, beating well after each addition. Beat in the orange zest, lemon zest, lemon juice, lavender, and vanilla.

Beginning with the dry ingredients, alternately beat in the flour and the buttermilk in three additions each. Stir in the crystallized ginger and poppy seeds.

Using an ice cream scoop, scoop out the batter into the muffin cups until three-quarters full. Bake for 12 to 15 minutes, or until light gold and springy to the touch. Let cool in the pan on a wire rack for 10 minutes, then transfer the cupcakes to the rack to cool completely.

Bake more batches to use all the batter.

Frost each cupcake with 2 tablespoons of the frosting and sprinkle with the sugar crystals.

Lavender-colored sparkling sugar crystals are available at stores that carry cake-decorating supplies.

Lavender Cream Cheese Frosting

1 (8-ounce) package plus 1
  (3-ounce) package cream
  cheese, at room temperature
$\frac{1}{2}$ pound (2 sticks) unsalted butter,
  at room temperature
2 teaspoons grated lemon zest
3 tablespoons fresh lemon juice
1 tablespoon dried culinary
  'Provence' lavender buds, finely
  ground in a spice grinder
$1\frac{1}{4}$ teaspoons vanilla extract
$4\frac{3}{4}$ cups confectioners' sugar, sifted

In a large bowl, combine the cream cheese, butter, lemon zest, lemon juice, lavender, and vanilla. Beat with an electric mixer until smooth. On low speed, gradually beat in the confectioners' sugar and continue beating until smooth.

Chocolate Meringue Nests
with Strawberry Margarita Compote

Whip up this light dessert for a party—or a special guest. The crunchy chocolate-lavender nests are the perfect counterpart to the slightly tart berry compote. Every time I make this recipe, it reminds me of my travels in the south of France during the Easter holiday.

To assure success when beating egg whites, make sure the bowl and beaters are very clean and free of any grease that would prevent the whites from achieving their full volume.

Meringue nests can be made days ahead and stored in an airtight container. If they begin to soften because of humidity, place them in a 200°F oven for 15 to 20 minutes to dry them out.

MAKES 6 SERVINGS

4 large egg whites, at room
  temperature
¹⁄₈ teaspoon cream of tartar
Pinch of salt
1 cup sugar
¹⁄₂ teaspoon vanilla extract
2 tablespoons unsweetened Dutch-
  process cocoa powder (see note)
1 teaspoon dried culinary
  'Provence' lavender buds, finely
  ground in a spice grinder
Strawberry Margarita Compote
  (recipe follows)
1 cup heavy cream
1 tablespoon confectioners' sugar
1 teaspoon vanilla extract
1 ounce semisweet baking chocolate,
  shaved into curls with a
  vegetable peeler
Fresh mint sprigs (garnish)

Preheat the oven to 200°F. Line a baking sheet with parchment paper and draw six 3-inch circles on the paper; turn the paper over so the ink or pencil marks are on the underside.

Place the egg whites, cream of tartar, and salt in a large bowl. Beat with an electric mixer on medium speed until foamy. Increase the speed to high and beat in the sugar 1 teaspoon at a time. Beat until the whites form stiff peaks when the beater is pulled out of the bowl. Beat in the vanilla.

Sift together the cocoa and lavender. Using a large rubber spatula, gently fold the mixture into the beaten whites until no streaks of white remain. Place the mixture in a pastry bag fitted with a large star tip. Pipe a layer of meringue to cover each drawn circle and form a base for the nests. Pipe at least 2 layers of meringue around the edges to build up sides on the nests. Bake for 2 hours, or until the nests are dry and stiff. Transfer the baking sheet to a wire rack and allow the nests to cool completely. Remove the nests from the paper.

While the nests bake, prepare the strawberry compote.

In a large bowl, combine the cream, confectioners' sugar, and vanilla. Beat with an electric mixer until stiff. Spoon or pipe half of the whipped cream into the nests. Top with the strawberries and then the remaining whipped cream. Top with chocolate curls. Serve immediately or refrigerate for up to 1 hour. Garnish with mint sprigs just before serving.

Dutch-process cocoa has been treated with an alkali to neutralize cocoa's natural acidity. It tends to be darker and richer than regular cocoa. Look for it in the baking aisle with other cocoa powder.

STRAWBERRY MARGARITA COMPOTE

½ cup Lavender Sugar (page 19, see note)
6 tablespoons orange liqueur
⅓ cup fresh lime juice
¼ cup finely chopped crystallized ginger
3½ tablespoons tequila
2 tablespoons grated orange zest
7 cups quartered strawberries

In a large bowl, whisk together the sugar, liqueur, lime juice, ginger, tequila, and orange zest. Add the strawberries and toss gently to combine. Let stand at room temperature for 1 hour or refrigerate for up to 4 hours.

If you don't have lavender sugar on hand, you can quickly make some. For this recipe, measure out ½ cup granulated sugar and transfer about 1 tablespoon to a spice grinder. Add ¾ teaspoon dried culinary 'Provence' lavender buds and pulse until the lavender is finely ground. Mix with the remaining sugar.

Old-Fashioned Cherry Pie with Lavender

Grandma would approve! This version features lavender in both the crust and filling, making an all-time favorite even better—and perfuming the kitchen with the most enticing aromas. To gild the lily, serve with Lavender Honey Custard Ice Cream (page 140).

MAKES 6 SERVINGS

Lavender Pie Dough (recipe follows)
1 cup plus 2 tablespoons
    granulated sugar
¼ cup quick-cooking tapioca
1 tablespoon dried 'Provence'
    lavender buds, finely ground
    in a spice grinder
½ teaspoon salt
½ teaspoon ground cinnamon
6 cups pitted fresh or frozen cherries
2 tablespoons vanilla extract
1 tablespoon Lavender Sugar
    (page 19)

Prepare the pie dough and refrigerate for 1 hour.

Preheat the oven to 375°F.

In a small bowl, stir together the granulated sugar, tapioca, lavender, salt, and cinnamon.

Place the cherries in a large saucepan and stir over medium-high heat for 5 minutes, or until slightly softened. Using a slotted spoon, transfer the cherries to a large bowl. Add the sugar mixture to the cherry juices in the pan and simmer, stirring, for 3 to 5 minutes, or until thickened. Pour over the cherries, add the vanilla, and stir to mix. Let cool.

On a lightly floured surface, roll one piece of dough into an 11-inch round (about ⅛ inch thick). Fit the dough into a 9-inch pie plate, leaving a ¾-inch overhang. Pour in the filling, cover loosely with plastic wrap, and chill.

Roll the remaining dough into an 11-inch round and use a sharp knife or fluted pastry wheel to cut it into 1-inch-wide strips. Working on a sheet of parchment paper set on a baking sheet, weave the pastry strips in a close lattice pattern. Refrigerate or freeze the lattice for 20 minutes, or until firm.

Brush the edge of the filled shell with cold water and slide the lattice off the parchment and onto the pie. Let stand for 10 minutes to soften the lattice. Trim the edges flush with the rim of the pie plate and crimp decoratively. Gently brush the lattice top with cold water and sprinkle with lavender sugar.

Bake in the middle of the oven for 50 to 60 minutes, or until the pastry is golden and the filling bubbles. Transfer to a wire rack to cool slightly. Serve warm.

If you're using fresh cherries, you'll need about 2 pounds.

LAVENDER PIE DOUGH

2½ cups all-purpose flour

1 tablespoon sugar

1 tablespoon dried culinary
'Provence' lavender buds, finely
ground in a spice grinder

1 teaspoon salt

¼ pound (1 stick) cold unsalted
butter, cut into pieces

½ cup shortening, chilled and
cut into pieces

¼ cup cold water

In the bowl of a food processor, combine the flour, sugar, lavender, and salt. Pulse to mix. Scatter the butter and shortening over the flour and pulse until the mixture resembles coarse crumbs; do not overprocess. Add the water and pulse until the dough starts to clump; if the dough is not clumping, add water 1 tablespoon at a time. Gather the dough into a ball and divide in half. Flatten each piece into a disk and wrap in plastic wrap. Refrigerate for 1 hour.

SUMMER LAVENDER

Sumptuous, Light, and Cooling

CONTENTS

SHRIMP WITH LAVENDER HONEY MARINADE

There are few dishes more welcoming than a platter of well-seasoned shrimp. This recipe is fast, easy, and filled with the sunny flavors of Provence. It makes a great do-ahead course. Lavender honey may be difficult to find, but regular honey works almost as well in this recipe.

MAKES 8 TO 10 SERVINGS

Marinade

½ cup lavender honey or honey
¼ cup dried culinary 'Provence' lavender buds, finely ground in a spice grinder
2 tablespoons extra-virgin olive oil
1½ tablespoons white wine vinegar
1 tablespoon fresh lemon juice
1 tablespoon fresh lime juice
1 tablespoon fresh tangerine juice
1 garlic clove, minced
Sea salt and freshly ground black pepper

Shrimp

5 cups water
1½ cups dry white wine
1 medium onion, quartered
½ lemon, sliced
½ lime, sliced
½ tangerine, sliced
1 tablespoon whole black peppercorns
1 tablespoon sea salt
1 bay leaf
⅛ teaspoon crushed hot-pepper flakes
2 pounds large shrimp (16 to 20 per pound), shelled with tail left on
Fresh lavender sprigs (garnish)

To make the marinade: In a small bowl, whisk together the honey, lavender, oil, vinegar, lemon juice, lime juice, tangerine juice, and garlic. Season with salt and pepper.

To make the shrimp: In a large pot, combine the water, wine, onion, lemon, lime, tangerine, peppercorns, salt, bay leaf, and pepper flakes. Bring to a boil over medium-high heat and boil for 5 minutes. Reduce the heat to medium, add the shrimp, and cook for 2 minutes, or until the shrimp have turned pink and are cooked through. Drain and transfer just the shrimp to a large bowl. Let cool for 5 minutes. Add the marinade and toss to combine. Let cool completely. Cover and refrigerate for 8 hours or overnight.

Transfer the shrimp to a serving platter and garnish with the lavender sprigs. Let stand at room temperature for 20 minutes before serving.

DRIED APRICOTS WITH LAVENDER GOAT CHEESE
AND PISTACHIOS

Nuts and cheese are staple hors d'oeuvres. Here's how to turn them into something really imaginative. Dried apricots serve as the base for the other ingredients, forming pretty—and healthy—appetizers. These may be prepared in advance and refrigerated, covered with plastic wrap. Allow them to stand at room temperature for 30 minutes before serving.

MAKES ABOUT 40 SERVINGS

½ pound dried apricot halves
   (about 40)
¼ cup orange juice
¼ cup bourbon or apricot brandy
1 (12-ounce) log soft mild goat
   cheese
2 tablespoons cranberry chutney
   or fig or plum jam
1 teaspoon dried culinary
   'Provence' lavender buds, finely
   ground in a spice grinder
¾ cup unsalted pistachio nuts,
   toasted and coarsely chopped

In a medium saucepan, combine the apricots, orange juice, and bourbon or brandy. Simmer over medium heat for 10 minutes, or until the apricots are soft and plump (stir occasionally and add more orange juice if the liquid boils away). Drain on paper towels and pat dry. Line a baking sheet with parchment paper and spread the apricots, cut side up, on the sheet.

In a food processor, blend the goat cheese, chutney or jam, and lavender. Transfer to a pastry bag fitted with a large plain or star tip. Pipe a small dollop of the mixture onto each apricot and sprinkle with the pistachios.

To insure that you get moist, beautiful-looking apricots, avoid those sold in boxes or bags that you can't see through. Turkish apricots are usually sold pitted but whole, so you'll need to separate the halves. California apricots are already halved. If you use very soft apricots, you may omit the cooking step.

Petite Bites of Salmon

with Orange-Miso Sauce

Everyone likes salmon, so serve up these grilled Asian treats at your next summer party. They can be readied ahead and grilled just before serving. You'll be surprised how lavender enhances the flavor of the salmon.

Be sure to use Asian (dark) sesame seed oil, which is very flavorful. Look for it—as well as miso, garlic chile paste, and black sesame seeds—at Japanese markets, natural food stores, and supermarkets with a well-stocked Asian foods section.

MAKES 24 SERVINGS

Orange-Miso Sauce (recipe follows)
1 pound skinless salmon fillet
(½ inch thick)
½ cup orange marmalade
½ cup frozen orange juice
concentrate, thawed
2 tablespoons Asian sesame oil
1 tablespoon grated fresh ginger
1 teaspoon dried culinary
'Provence' lavender buds, finely
ground in a spice grinder
Sea salt and freshly ground black
pepper
1 cup white or black sesame seeds

Prepare the sauce.

Cut the salmon crosswise into strips about the width and length of your index finger.

In a large bowl, mix the marmalade, juice concentrate, oil, ginger, and lavender. Add the salmon and toss to coat. Season with salt and pepper.

Place the sesame seeds on a small plate. Coat the salmon pieces lightly with the seeds. Arrange the salmon in a single layer on a baking sheet. Cover and chill for at least 2 hours or up to 8 hours.

Soak a package of 6-inch bamboo skewers in water for 30 minutes, then drain. Preheat a grill to medium-hot.

Thread each salmon strip onto 2 skewers placed ¼ inch apart (the double skewers prevent the fish from twirling during grilling, making it easier to turn). Grill the skewers for 3 minutes per side, or until the salmon is cooked through. Transfer to a serving platter. Serve warm with the sauce.

ORANGE-MISO SAUCE

1 cup mayonnaise
2 tablespoons frozen orange juice
   concentrate, thawed
1 tablespoon yellow miso
   (fermented soybean paste)
1 tablespoon Asian sesame oil
1 teaspoon dried culinary
   'Provence' lavender buds, finely
   ground in a spice grinder
1 tablespoon minced garlic
1 tablespoon garlic chile paste
1 teaspoon grated fresh ginger
1/2 teaspoon grated orange zest
Sea salt and freshly ground black
   pepper

In a medium bowl, whisk together the mayonnaise, juice concentrate, miso, oil, lavender, garlic, chile paste, ginger, and orange zest. Season with salt and pepper. Cover and refrigerate until needed.

Santa Fe Lavender Chile Torta

This is perfect party food. Serve the layered cheese "cake" with crunchy tortilla or pita chips for scooping.

MAKES 10 TO 12 SERVINGS

1 cup finely crushed avocado or lime tortilla chips

3 tablespoons unsalted butter, melted

1 (8-ounce) package cream cheese, at room temperature

8 ounces fresh goat cheese, at room temperature

2 large eggs

8 ounces Monterey Jack cheese, shredded

1 (4-ounce) can chopped mild green chile peppers, drained

1 tablespoon Spiced Lavender Seasoning (page 18)

Hot-pepper sauce

1 cup sour cream, at room temperature

1 tablespoon fresh lime juice

1 cup chopped orange or yellow bell pepper

½ cup sliced green onion

⅓ cup chopped Roma (Italian) tomato

¼ cup sliced California black olives

Preheat the oven to 325°F.

In a small bowl, mix the chips and butter. Press into the bottom and up the sides of a 9-inch springform pan. Bake for 15 minutes. Set aside.

In a large bowl, combine the cream cheese, goat cheese, and eggs. Beat with an electric mixer until well blended. Mix in the Monterey Jack, chile peppers, lavender seasoning, and a dash of pepper sauce. Pour into the springform pan and bake for 30 minutes. The mixture should be slightly firm in the center when you touch it and jiggle a little in the center.

In a small bowl, mix the sour cream and lime juice. Spread evenly over the warm torta. Set on a wire rack to cool completely. Cover the pan with plastic wrap and refrigerate for at least 2 hours or up to 2 days.

Just before serving, run a thin-bladed knife around the edge of the pan to loosen the sides. Remove the rim from the springform pan and place the torta on a serving plate. To decorate the top: Place a circle of bell pepper around the outer edge. Follow with an inner circle of green onion. Fill the center with tomato and olives.

To make the most of green onions, include the tender green tops when chopping them.

LIGURIAN FOCACCIA
WITH CARAMELIZED ONIONS AND OLIVE TAPENADE

A favorite of my students, this bread was inspired by one of my trips to Liguria, Italy, with the Oldways Preservation Trust—an organization dedicated to preserving the old ways of growing, preparing, and eating food. The lavender and rosemary are my additions to an old Italian recipe.

MAKES 8 SERVINGS

1 cup warm water (105° to 115°F)
1 tablespoon active dried yeast
1½ cups water, at room temperature
1 tablespoon finely chopped fresh
    rosemary leaves
2 teaspoons dried culinary
    'Provence' lavender buds, finely
    ground in a spice grinder
½ cup extra-virgin olive oil
Sea salt
8 cups all-purpose flour
Caramelized Onions and Olive
    Tapenade (recipe follows)
8 ounces Taleggio, Teleme, or ripe
    Brie cheese, rind removed

Place the warm water in a large bowl and sprinkle with the yeast. Let stand for 5 minutes, or until foamy. Stir in the room-temperature water, rosemary, lavender, ¼ cup of the oil, and 1 tablespoon salt. Work in the flour a little at a time, adding just enough to make a dough that does not stick to the sides of the bowl (you may not need the whole amount). Turn the dough out onto a floured surface and knead energetically for 5 to 8 minutes, or until smooth and elastic.

Lightly oil a bowl, place the dough in it, and turn to coat the top with oil. Cover with plastic wrap, set in a warm place, and let rise until doubled in size, about 1 hour.

Prepare the tapenade mixture.

Punch down the dough and cut it in half. Generously oil a 17 x 11-inch jelly-roll pan. Place one piece of dough in the pan and push it with your fingers until it extends to the sides of the pan. If the dough is too elastic, let it rest for 5 minutes before continuing. On a lightly floured surface, roll the second piece of dough to the same size as the pan and set aside.

Drop small spoonfuls of the cheese over the surface of the dough in the pan. Cover with the rolled dough. Pinch the edges to seal the pieces. Dimple the dough with your fingers. Spoon the remaining ¼ cup olive oil and the tapenade mixture evenly over the top. (The dimples will catch the oil as the dough bakes.) Cover loosely with plastic wrap, set in a warm place, and let rise for 40 minutes.

Preheat the oven to 475°F. Bake the focaccia on the bottom rack for 15 minutes, or until golden and still a little soft. Serve hot or at room temperature. Cut into squares.

CARAMELIZED ONIONS AND OLIVE TAPENADE

3 tablespoons extra-virgin olive oil
2 medium red onions, thinly sliced
1 tablespoon water
2 tablespoons balsamic vinegar
2 teaspoons dried culinary
  'Provence' lavender buds, finely
ground in a spice grinder
¾ cup black or green olive tapenade
Sea salt and freshly ground black
  pepper

Warm the oil in a large skillet over medium heat. Add the onions and water. Sauté, stirring frequently, for 10 to 15 minutes, or until deep golden brown. Remove from the heat and stir in the vinegar and lavender. Let cool. Stir in the tapenade and season with salt and pepper.

Summer Lavender Raspberry Oat Muffins

Wake up and taste these go-getter muffins. Luscious summer fruit contrasts well with the sweetly spiced topping. For variety, replace the raspberries with a diced peach. Or use ½ cup raspberries and half a peach.

MAKES 12 MUFFINS

Topping

⅓ cup firmly packed light brown
    sugar
1 tablespoon all-purpose flour
1 tablespoon unsalted butter,
    at room temperature
1 teaspoon dried culinary
    'Provence' lavender buds, finely
    ground in a spice grinder
½ teaspoon ground cinnamon

Muffins

½ cup rolled oats
½ cup orange juice
½ cup vegetable oil
1 egg, slightly beaten
1½ cups all-purpose flour
½ cup sugar
2 teaspoons dried culinary
    'Provence' lavender buds, finely
    ground in a spice grinder
1½ teaspoons baking powder
1½ teaspoons baking soda
½ teaspoon salt
1 cup fresh raspberries

Preheat the oven to 425°F. Grease and flour 12 muffin cups or line with papers.

To make the topping: In a small bowl, mix the brown sugar, flour, butter, lavender, and cinnamon until crumbly.

To make the muffins: In a large bowl, mix the oats and orange juice. Stir in the oil and egg. Add the flour, sugar, lavender, baking powder, baking soda, and salt. Mix well. Gently fold in the raspberries.

Spoon into the prepared baking cups, filling them about two-thirds. Sprinkle with the topping.

Bake for 18 to 22 minutes, or until lightly golden. Cool on a wire rack for 10 minutes before removing from the pan. Serve warm or at room temperature.

LAVENDER GINGER LEMONADE

Nothing is more invigorating than a glass of cold lemonade on a hot day. Lavender and ginger transform an old favorite into an exquisite refreshment. This is the perfect beverage for tea parties and other festive summer occasions. For something more adult, add a little vodka or gin.

The Lavender Ginger Syrup is also the base for Lavender Guava Wine Cooler (page 74).

MAKES 6 SERVINGS

Lavender Ginger Syrup (recipe
   follows)
4 cups water
½ cup fresh lemon juice

Prepare the lavender syrup.

In a 2-quart pitcher, combine the water, lemon juice, and syrup. Add ice to the top and stir to chill (or serve in ice-filled glasses).

LAVENDER GINGER SYRUP

I cup sugar
4 ounces crystallized ginger, chopped
2 tablespoons dried culinary
   'Provence' lavender buds
Grated zest of 2 lemons
2 cups water

In a food processor, combine the sugar, ginger, lavender, and lemon zest. Blend for I minute, or until the ginger is broken into small pieces. Transfer to a medium saucepan and add the water. Bring to a boil and cook for I minute. Strain into a bowl and discard the solids.

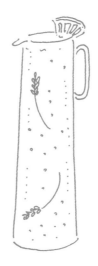

Lavender Guava Wine Cooler

What a refreshing change of pace! Your guests will enjoy this drink so much that you'd better plan on making extra.

MAKES 12 SERVINGS

3 cups canned guava nectar, chilled
1 (750-milliliter) bottle white
    Zinfandel wine, chilled
2 cups Lavender Ginger Syrup
    (page 73)
1 (25-ounce) bottle sparkling
    water, chilled

In a 3-quart pitcher, mix the guava nectar, wine, and syrup. Just before serving, gently stir in the sparkling water. Add ice to the top and stir to chill (or serve in ice-filled glasses).

Lavender Margaritas

South of France meets south of the border! Whip up a batch of the Lavender Sweet and Sour Mix and keep it in the fridge for up to a week. When you want margaritas, just add tequila and Triple Sec or other orange liqueur. Serve over ice or turn into a slush in the blender.

You can also use the sweet and sour mix for other drinks. Mix it with your choice of alcohol and plenty of ice.

MAKES 10 TO 12 SERVINGS

Lavender Sweet and Sour Mix
    (recipe follows)
1¼ cups tequila
¾ cup orange liqueur
1 lime
½ cup Lavender Salt Dry Rub
    (page 17)

Prepare the sweet and sour mix.

In a large pitcher, combine the mix, tequila, and liqueur. Add ice.

Cut the lime into wedges and use to rub the rims of margarita glasses. Dip into the lavender salt. Fill with the tequila mixture.

Lavender Sweet and Sour Mix

3 cups sugar

2 cups water

1 tablespoon dried culinary
'Provence' lavender buds

2 cups fresh lime juice

2 cups fresh lemon juice

In a medium saucepan, mix the sugar, water, and lavender. Bring to a boil over high heat and stir to dissolve the sugar. Cover, remove from the heat, and let steep for 5 minutes. Strain into a pitcher or large jar. Add the lime juice and lemon juice. Cover and refrigerate until cold.

Lavender Tangerine Mimosas

Start any brunch off with this truly delicious combination of lavender, tangerine juice, Triple Sec and bubbly Champagne. Delightfully straying from the classic mimosa, this new twist on the old will have your guests asking for more. Be forewarned, they go down easy.

MAKES 6 TO 8 SERVINGS

¼ cup orange liqueur

¼ cup Lavender Syrup (page 20)

2½ cups fresh tangerine juice

1 (750-milliliter) bottle dry
Champagne, chilled

In a large pitcher, mix the liqueur, lavender syrup, and tangerine juice. Gently pour in the Champagne and stir to combine.

Cold Cantaloupe Soup
with Yogurt Lime Cream and Lavender

This refreshing soup represents summer itself—full of ripe fruit and sweet wine. A touch of lavender provides an herbal note to this cool pick-me-up.

MAKES 6 TO 8 SERVINGS

1 cantaloupe (about 3 pounds),
    seeded, peeled, and cut into
    large cubes
2 pounds frozen yellow peaches,
    diced
1 cup fresh tangerine or orange
    juice
½ cup fresh lime juice
1 tablespoon honey or lavender
    honey
1 (8-ounce) container plain yogurt
1 cup sweet wine, such as
    Riesling or Gewürztraminer
2 tablespoons lime zest
1 tablespoon dried culinary
    'Provence' lavender buds,
    crushed or finely ground in
    a spice grinder

Place the cantaloupe in a blender and blend until fairly smooth (if necessary, work in batches). Add the peaches and blend until fairly smooth. Add the tangerine or orange juice, lime juice, honey, and 2 tablespoons of the yogurt. Blend until smooth. Pour into a large bowl and stir in the wine. Cover with plastic wrap and refrigerate for at least 3 hours or up to 24 hours.

In a small bowl, mix the lime zest with the remaining yogurt. Cover and refrigerate until needed.

Ladle the soup into chilled bowls and garnish with a dollop of the yogurt mixture. Sprinkle with the lavender.

Cold Cucumber Soup
with Stuffed Zucchini Blossoms

This cold soup is dressed to impress! Zucchini blossoms take the presentation "over the top."
Get a head start on this soup by preparing the yogurt cheese the day before.

MAKES 8 SERVINGS

1 (16-ounce) container plain
   yogurt (see note)
3 English cucumbers (3½ pounds),
   peeled and thickly sliced
1 cup chicken broth, chilled
6 green onions, diced
3 tablespoons rice wine vinegar
Sea salt
2 tablespoons dried culinary
   'Provence' lavender buds, finely
   ground in a spice grinder
2 avocados
2 teaspoons wasabi paste
1 tablespoon grated lime zest
¼ cup fresh lime juice
Freshly ground black pepper
8 large zucchini blossoms
¼ cup chopped chives

Line a strainer or colander with a double thickness of cheesecloth or a paper coffee filter. Add the yogurt. Place over a bowl, cover with plastic wrap, and refrigerate for 8 hours or overnight, until the yogurt drains and becomes very thick. Discard the liquid that drips into the bowl.

In a food processor, combine the cucumbers, broth, green onions, vinegar, 1 teaspoon salt, and 1 tablespoon of the lavender. Halve, pit, peel, and chop 1 avocado; add to the food processor. Blend until smooth.

Reserve ¼ cup of the yogurt cheese; add the remainder to the food processor. Add the wasabi, lime zest, and lime juice. Blend until smooth. Season with salt and pepper. Cover and refrigerate for at least 6 hours or up to 24 hours.

Gently open the zucchini blossoms and remove the yellow stamens. Cut off any spiky leaves at the base of the blossoms.

Halve, pit, and peel the remaining avocado. Dice it and place in a small bowl. Stir in the reserved yogurt cheese and the remaining 1 tablespoon lavender. Season with salt and pepper. Use a small spoon to fill the blossoms with the mixture. Gently twist the tips of the blossoms around the filling. Set on a baking sheet, cover, and refrigerate until firm.

Ladle the soup into soup bowls. Set a stuffed blossom in the center of each bowl. Sprinkle with the chives.

When making yogurt cheese, use natural yogurt, which contains no thickeners such as gelatin. Thickeners prevent the liquid whey in the yogurt from draining off, and the yogurt will not thicken to a cream cheese consistency.

GRILLED LAVENDER SEAFOOD SALAD
WITH PACIFIC RIM DRESSING

Wandering through an Australian lavender farm one October, I was inspired to create the perfect Down Under seafood salad with coconut and lavender essence. This exotic scallop and shrimp dish was the result. It's ideal for summer buffets, picnics, and beach excursions. Serve it on a scalloped or shell-shaped platter for the biggest impact.

When preparing scallops, always use fairly high heat to cook them quickly. They should be seared on the outside, hot on the inside, opaque throughout, and very tender. Overcooking turns scallops rubbery.

MAKES 6 SERVINGS

Scallops
1 tablespoon coriander seeds
1 tablespoon dried culinary
 'Provence' lavender buds
1 cup tequila
1 cup unsweetened coconut milk
1 tablespoon grated lime zest
¼ cup fresh lime juice
1 pound large sea scallops
¼ cup finely chopped green onion

Salad
Pacific Rim Dressing
 (recipe follows)
½ pound cooked bay shrimp
 (see note)
1 large ripe papaya, seeded,
 peeled, and diced
½ cup finely chopped celery
½ cup finely grated fresh coconut
½ cup sliced (on the diagonal)
 green onion
½ cup julienned red bell pepper
½ pound baby spinach
1 starfruit, sliced (garnish)
1 kiwifruit, peeled and cut into
 wedges (garnish)

To make the scallops: Toast the coriander seeds in a dry skillet over medium heat until fragrant, about 2 minutes. Transfer to a spice grinder and add the lavender. Pulse until finely ground. Transfer to a medium bowl and whisk in the tequila, coconut milk, lime zest, and lime juice. Stir in the scallops and green onion. Cover and refrigerate for 1 hour.

Preheat a grill to medium-high. Drain the scallops well and place in a grilling basket. Grill, occasionally shaking the basket to turn the scallops, for 4 minutes, or until just opaque. Transfer the scallops to a bowl and set aside to cool. When cool, cut the scallops in half.

To make the salad: Prepare the dressing.

In a large bowl, combine the shrimp, papaya, celery, coconut, green onion, and pepper. Add the scallops and dressing. Toss to mix well. Arrange the spinach on a platter. Top with the salad. Garnish with the starfruit and kiwifruit.

Bay shrimp are very small shrimp and number 250 to 350 per pound.

Pacific Rim Dressing

1 (15-ounce) can unsweetened
    coconut milk
½ cup sour cream
½ cup mango chutney
1 tablespoon grated lime zest
1 tablespoon fresh lime juice
1 tablespoon grated fresh ginger
1 tablespoon dried culinary
    'Provence' lavender buds, finely
    ground in a spice grinder
1 tablespoon honey mustard
Sea salt and freshly ground black
    pepper

In a blender, combine the coconut milk, sour cream, chutney, lime zest, lime juice, ginger, lavender, and mustard. Blend until smooth and creamy. Season with salt and pepper.

Salad of Roasted Ratatouille
and Lavender Goat Cheese with Herb Vinaigrette

Enjoy the aromatic flavors of the Mediterranean in this colorful salad. The lavender-scented goat cheese adds protein as well as creaminess, making this perfect luncheon fare for country picnics and poolside parties.

By all means, save the oil from the goat cheese marinade to flavor other recipes. Store it in the refrigerator.

MAKES 8 SERVINGS

Lavender-Marinated Goat Cheese
(recipe follows)
1 pound Italian (baby) eggplants
Sea salt
½ cup extra-virgin olive oil
2 small zucchini, diced
1 small yellow squash, diced
1 red bell pepper, julienned
1 yellow bell pepper, julienned
1 green bell pepper, julienned
1 medium red onion, diced
3 medium Roma (Italian)
    tomatoes, peeled, seeded,
    and diced
1 teaspoon minced garlic
¼ cup drained capers
3 tablespoons fresh Italian parsley
    leaves, minced
1 tablespoon dried basil
1 tablespoon fresh thyme leaves
Freshly ground black pepper
Herb Vinaigrette (recipe follows)
1 pound mixed baby greens

Prepare the goat cheese and marinate overnight.

Trim the eggplants but do not peel. Cut into small cubes. Sprinkle generously with salt and place in a colander to drain for 1 hour. Rinse with cold water and pat dry with paper towels.

Preheat the oven to 375°F.

In a large bowl, gently toss the eggplant with ¼ cup of the oil and spread evenly on a rimmed baking sheet. Roast, stirring often, for 30 minutes, or until tender.

In the same bowl, mix the zucchini, yellow squash, red pepper, yellow pepper, green pepper, onion, tomatoes, garlic, and the remaining ¼ cup olive oil. Add to the eggplant and roast, stirring often, for 20 minutes longer, or until lightly browned. Transfer to a clean bowl. Stir in the capers, parsley, basil, and thyme. Season with salt and pepper.

Prepare the vinaigrette. Pour half over the vegetables and toss to combine.

Arrange the greens around the outside of a serving platter. Mound the vegetables in the center. Drizzle with the remaining vinaigrette. Remove the goat cheese balls from the oil and scatter over the salad.

Lavender–Marinated Goat Cheese

1 (12-ounce) log soft goat cheese
2 cups extra-virgin olive oil
2 tablespoons dried culinary
'Provence' lavender buds, finely
ground in a spice grinder

Cut the goat cheese into 1-inch pieces and roll each into a ball. In a 1-quart jar, mix the oil and lavender. Immerse the balls in the oil. Cover and refrigerate overnight.

Herb Vinaigrette

1½ tablespoons sherry vinegar
1½ teaspoons dried basil
1½ teaspoons minced garlic
1½ teaspoons minced shallot
1 tablespoon grated Parmesan
cheese
1 tablespoon pine nuts, toasted
¾ cup lavender olive oil
(from goat cheese marinade)
Sea salt and freshly ground black
pepper

In a blender, combine vinegar, basil, garlic, shallot, cheese, and pine nuts. Add ¾ cup oil from the goat cheese marinade. Blend until smooth. Season with salt and pepper.

Spinach and Endive Salad
with Lavender Lemon-Ginger Dressing

When succulent fruit is in season, be sure to add some to your green salads. This salad pairs a spicy-tart dressing, peaches, and blueberries with slightly bitter greens. It's a good accompaniment to grilled meat or chicken. For an extra bit of crunch and sweetness, sprinkle the salad with Rosemary's Spiced Lavender Walnuts (page 105).

MAKES 4 SERVINGS

Lavender Lemon-Ginger Dressing
   (recipe follows)
2 medium peaches
2 Belgian endives
4 cups packed baby spinach
I cup blueberries
I tablespoon chopped chives

Prepare the dressing and cool to room temperature.

Peel, pit, and slice the peaches. Place in a small bowl and add half of the dressing. Toss to combine.

Halve the endives and cut lengthwise into long slivers. Place in a large bowl and add the spinach. Add the remaining dressing and toss to coat. Transfer to a serving platter and arrange the peach slices decoratively over the greens. Sprinkle with the blueberries and chives.

Lavender Lemon-Ginger Dressing

¾ cup extra-virgin olive oil
½ cup white wine vinegar
I tablespoon fresh lemon juice
I tablespoon grated fresh ginger
I tablespoon apple jelly
½ teaspoon Dijon mustard
I teaspoon dried culinary
   'Provence' lavender buds, finely
   ground in a spice grinder

In a small saucepan, combine the oil, vinegar, lemon juice, ginger, jelly, and mustard. Whisk over low heat until the dressing is warmed through and completely blended. Cool to room temperature and stir in the lavender.

Lavender Beet, Bean, and Shallot Salad

Beets add deep color and hearty flavor to this summer salad. Roasting brings out their sweetness, which provides a delightful counterpoint to the piquant dressing.

MAKES 6 TO 8 SERVINGS

Beets

2 pounds small beets, with 1 inch
    of stems remaining
3 tablespoons extra-virgin olive oil
2 tablespoons dried culinary
    'Provence' lavender buds, finely
    ground in a spice grinder

Salad

1 pound tender green beans
1 pound tender yellow beans
¾ cup plus 2 tablespoons
    extra-virgin olive oil
½ cup red wine vinegar
1 teaspoon dried culinary
    'Provence' lavender buds, finely
    ground in a spice grinder
Sea salt and freshly ground black
    pepper
4 shallots, thinly sliced
¼ cup chopped fresh basil leaves
1 tablespoon chopped chives

To make the beets: Preheat the oven to 375°F.

Place the beets on a large sheet of foil and sprinkle with the oil and lavender; toss to combine. Fold up the foil to make a sealed packet. (If necessary, make 2 packets.) Place on a baking sheet.

Roast for 30 to 45 minutes, or until tender when tested with a sharp knife. Set aside until cool enough to handle. Slip off the skins. Thinly slice the beets crosswise and let cool.

To make the salad: Bring a large pot of water to a boil. Add the green beans and yellow beans and cook for 5 to 6 minutes, or until tender but still crunchy. Drain and transfer to a large bowl of cold water and ice cubes to cool. Drain and pat dry with paper towels.

In a large bowl, whisk together the oil, vinegar, and lavender. Season with salt and pepper. Add the beets, beans, shallots, basil, and chives. Toss to combine. Transfer to a platter.

The roasted beets can be prepared up to a day ahead; cover and refrigerate.

California Lavender Pasta Salad

This very healthy salad is a breeze to prepare. You can make it ahead, so it's ideal for busy days. The broccoli will discolor if it's in contact with the dressing for too long, so add it right before serving.

MAKES 10 TO 12 SERVINGS

Lavender Dijon Dressing
(recipe follows)
1 small bunch broccoli
1 pound dry bow tie or ziti pasta
2 large red bell peppers, diced
2½ cups thinly sliced celery
1 red onion, thinly sliced
1 cup sliced California black olives
1 (10-ounce) package frozen
   artichoke hearts, thawed and
   quartered
½ cup oil-packed sun-dried
   tomatoes, blotted of excess oil
   and julienned
¼ cup fresh lemon thyme or
   thyme leaves
Sea salt and freshly ground black
   pepper

Prepare the dressing.

Cut the broccoli florets from the stems and reserve the stems for another use. Cut the florets into ½-inch pieces. Bring a large saucepan of water to a boil. Working in batches if necessary, cook the broccoli for 3 minutes, or until crisp-tender. Drain in a colander and run under cold water until cooled completely. Pat dry with paper towels and refrigerate until needed.

Cook the pasta in a large pot of boiling salted water according to the package directions, until just tender to the bite. Drain, transfer to a large bowl, and add half of the dressing. Toss well. Cover and refrigerate until cold.

Add the bell peppers, celery, onion, olives, artichokes, tomatoes, thyme, and the remaining dressing. Toss well and season with salt and pepper. Just before serving, stir in the broccoli.

Lavender Dijon Dressing

½ cup extra-virgin olive oil
2 tablespoons red wine vinegar
2 tablespoons Dijon mustard
2 teaspoons dried culinary
   'Provence' lavender buds, finely
   ground in a spice grinder
¾ teaspoon sea salt
½ teaspoon minced garlic
¼ teaspoon freshly ground black
   pepper

In a jar with a tight-fitting lid, combine the oil, vinegar, mustard, lavender, salt, garlic, and pepper. Shake well to combine.

GRILLED LAVENDER LAMB CHOPS

Lamb chops are quick and easy to prepare. This recipe will definitely raise the bar for barbecue fare!

MAKES 8 SERVINGS

¼ cup pomegranate molasses
    (see note)
¼ cup fresh lemon juice
2 tablespoons fresh lime juice
½ cup finely chopped white onion
2 garlic cloves, minced
2 teaspoons dried culinary
    'Provence' lavender buds, finely
    ground in a spice grinder
8 lamb chops, ¾ inch thick
Sea salt and freshly ground black
    pepper

In a small bowl, whisk together the molasses, lemon juice, lime juice, onion, garlic, and lavender. Sprinkle the chops with salt and pepper. Place in a single layer in a glass baking dish. Pour the marinade over the chops and turn to coat both sides. Cover and refrigerate, turning occasionally, for at least 1 hour or up to 4 hours. Bring the meat to room temperature before grilling.

Preheat a grill to medium. Grill the chops for 2 to 4 minutes per side, or until nicely seared on the outside and still pink on the inside (an internal temperature of 140°F).

Pomegranate molasses is available at most international and Middle Eastern food markets. You can also order it at www.deandeluca.com.

GRILLED LAVENDER HONEY BREAST OF CHICKEN

Grilled chicken meets a smashing combination of citrus, lavender, and honey. This is my version of a recipe created by my good friend Liz Clark, who taught a cooking class on a tour in Provence. If you're fortunate enough to find lavender wine vinegar, by all means use it. I got mine in the little town of Saint-Paul-de-Vence.

MAKES 8 SERVINGS

¾ cup white wine vinegar or
    lavender wine vinegar
¼ cup grated lemon zest
½ cup fresh lemon juice
¼ cup extra-virgin olive oil
¼ cup lavender honey or honey
1 tablespoon dried culinary
    'Provence' lavender buds, finely
    ground in a spice grinder
1½ teaspoons fresh lime juice
1 teaspoon sea salt
¼ tablespoon cracked black pepper
8 boneless chicken breast halves
    with skin

In a large bowl, mix the vinegar, lemon zest, lemon juice, oil, honey, lavender, lime juice, salt, and pepper. Add the chicken and turn to coat. Cover and refrigerate for 4 hours.

Preheat a grill to medium. Remove the chicken from the marinade and place, skin side down, on the grill. Cook, turning the chicken every 5 minutes and brushing occasionally with marinade, for 15 minutes, or until no longer pink when tested with a sharp knife. Discard any remaining marinade.

Spinach-Wrapped Sole,
Warm Lentil Salad, and Lavender Cucumber Sauce

This is so pretty you'll want to serve it to guests—but don't reserve it only for special occasions. It's perfect for an everyday light summer meal. Lavender and mint bring out the flavors of the fish and spinach.

MAKES 6 SERVINGS

Lavender Cucumber Sauce (recipe follows)
Warm Lentil Salad (recipe follows)
Sea salt
1½ pounds large spinach leaves, stems removed
6 (6-ounce) sole fillets
Freshly ground black pepper
¼ cup fresh mint leaves, finely chopped
2 tablespoons extra-virgin olive oil

Prepare the sauce and refrigerate until needed.

Prepare the lentils.

While the lentils cook, preheat the oven to 400°F. Line a baking sheet with a double layer of paper towels. Oil a rimmed baking sheet.

Bring a large pot of salted water to a boil. Drop a large handful of the spinach into the water, cook for 2 seconds, and remove with a slotted spoon. Transfer to the baking sheet lined with paper towels and smooth out the leaves so they lie flat. Repeat to use all the leaves; add more layers of paper towels, if needed.

Pat the sole dry with paper towels and season with salt and pepper. On the oiled rimmed baking sheet, overlap 5 or 6 spinach leaves to form a wrap. Place a fillet in the center, sprinkle with mint, and fold the spinach over the sole. Top with more spinach to completely encase the sole. Repeat to encase the remaining fillets.

Brush the tops with the oil. Bake for 10 minutes, or until the fish is opaque throughout when tested with a sharp knife.

Spoon the lentils onto a serving platter. Carefully transfer the sole with a spatula onto the top of the lentils. Spoon a little sauce over each fillet and serve immediately, passing the remaining sauce on the side.

Lavender Cucumber Sauce

2 garlic cloves
Sea salt
1 cup plain yogurt
1 tablespoon dried culinary
    'Provence' lavender buds, finely
    ground in a spice grinder
½ English cucumber, peeled,
    seeded, and thickly sliced
¼ cup fresh mint leaves, finely
    chopped
Freshly ground black pepper

Chop the garlic, sprinkle with ¼ teaspoon salt, and mince into a paste. Transfer to a small bowl and stir in the yogurt and lavender. Place the cucumber in a blender and blend until smooth. Stir into the yogurt mixture. Add the mint and season with salt and pepper. Cover and refrigerate until needed.

Warm Lentil Salad

1 cup green French lentils
    (see note)
1 tablespoon extra-virgin olive oil
1 red onion, diced
1 tablespoon red wine vinegar
Sea salt and freshly ground black
    pepper
½ cup crumbled feta cheese,
    preferably French

Place the lentils in a medium saucepan and cover with about 2 inches of water. Bring to a boil and cook for 30 minutes, or until tender; if needed, add more water as the lentils cook. Drain, rinse with cold water, and transfer to a medium bowl.

Warm the oil in a large skillet over medium heat. Add the onion and sauté until translucent, about 5 minutes. Add the lentils and vinegar. Season with salt and pepper. Simmer for 3 minutes. Remove from the heat, let cool for 10 minutes, and then stir in the cheese.

 If you soak the lentils in cold water overnight, you'll cut the cooking time in half and improve the texture.

CRISPY TEA-SMOKED DUCK BREAST
WITH BLUEBERRY SAUCE

This recipe may look formidable, but it's actually easy. Just take it a step at a time and you'll quickly transform plain duck breasts into a stellar dinner. The juxtaposition of sweet blueberries and mellow balsamic vinegar in the sauce creates the perfect accompaniment. You may make the sauce and smoke the duck up to 1 day ahead.

MAKES 4 SERVINGS

Marinade
1 cup Merlot wine
¼ cup extra-virgin olive oil
¼ cup sherry vinegar
3 tablespoons grated lemon zest
¼ cup fresh lemon juice
¼ cup fresh lime juice
2 tablespoons light or regular
    soy sauce
2 tablespoons minced fresh ginger
2 tablespoons minced garlic
1 teaspoon dried culinary
    'Provence' lavender buds, finely
    ground in a spice grinder

Duck
4 boneless duck breast halves
    (1½ pounds)
¼ cup uncooked long-grain
    white rice
¼ cup packed light brown sugar
¼ cup lavender black tea (see note)
2 tablespoons grated orange zest
Blueberry Sauce (recipe follows)
Sea salt and freshly ground black
    pepper
Fresh lavender sprigs (garnish)

To make the marinade: In a bowl, whisk together the wine, oil, vinegar, lemon zest, lemon juice, lime juice, soy sauce, ginger, garlic, and lavender.

To make the duck: Put the duck in a large resealable plastic bag, pour in the marinade, and seal the bag. Place the bag in a large bowl and refrigerate overnight, turning the bag occasionally.

Preheat a grill to high.

Line a wok with heavy-duty foil, leaving a few inches of foil overhanging the edges all around. Line the lid with foil, again leaving foil overhanging the edges; separate the foil from the lid.

In a small bowl, mix the rice, brown sugar, tea, and orange zest. Spread evenly in the wok. Oil a round cake rack or steamer rack that fits in the wok and sits about 1 inch above the rice mixture.

Remove the duck from the marinade and place, skin side up, on the rack. Set the wok on the stove over high heat. When the ingredients start to smoke in several places, place the piece of lid foil (dome up) over the wok. Tightly crimp the overhanging foil to establish a good seal. Cover with the wok lid. Smoke the duck for 10 minutes. Turn off the heat and let stand for 5 minutes.

While the duck smokes, prepare the blueberry sauce.

Take the wok outside. Use tongs or oven mitts to carefully undo the sealed foil and let the smoke escape; open the foil away from you. The duck should be mahogany in color.

Transfer the duck, skin side down, to the grill over indirect heat. Grill for 5 minutes to crisp the skin and produce grill marks. Season with salt and pepper. Slice the breasts crosswise, garnish with lavender sprigs, and serve with the sauce.

If you don't have lavender black tea, use ¼ cup black tea mixed with ¼ teaspoon ground dried 'Provence' lavender buds.

BLUEBERRY SAUCE

¼ cup sugar

2 tablespoons water

½ cup chicken broth

2½ tablespoons balsamic vinegar

1 tablespoon duck or veal
   demi-glace (see note)

1 teaspoon dried culinary
   'Provence' lavender buds, finely
   ground in a spice grinder

1 cup fresh or frozen blueberries

1 tablespoon minced fresh ginger

Combine the sugar and water in a small saucepan. Stir over low heat until the sugar dissolves. Stir in the broth, vinegar, demi-glace, lavender, and ¾ cup of the blueberries. Raise the heat to medium and cook for 10 minutes.

Using a handheld blender or a food processor, blend the sauce until smooth. Cook over high heat, stirring often, for 8 minutes, or until syrupy. Stir in the ginger and the remaining ¼ cup blueberries. Set aside or cover and refrigerate for up to 1 day.

Demi-glace is a very flavorful, reduced stock. It's available at many butcher shops and specialty food shops as well as from www.morethangourmet.com.

PROVENCE FETTUCCINE NUOVI

While traveling in the south of France, I ate at an incredible wine and pasta restaurant in the little town of Saint-Rémy. Back home, I recreated one of their dishes and enhanced it with lavender.

MAKES 8 SERVINGS

2 tablespoons unsalted butter

1 tablespoon diced shallot

2 garlic cloves, minced

2 ripe tomatoes, cubed

1 leek, julienned

2 teaspoons dried culinary 'Provence' lavender buds, finely ground

1/2 cup seedless green grapes

4 shiitake mushrooms, sliced

2 tablespoons Pernod liqueur

1 tablespoon chopped fresh basil leaves

1 tablespoon extra-virgin olive oil

1 cup heavy cream

1 cup tomato sauce

1 pound dry basil fettuccine

1 1/2 cups grated Parmesan cheese

1/4 cup fresh Italian parsley leaves, chopped

Melt the butter in a large skillet over medium-high heat. Add the shallot and garlic. Cook, stirring, for 3 minutes, or until golden. Stir in the tomatoes, leek, lavender, grapes, mushrooms, and Pernod.

Using a mortar and pestle, crush together the basil and oil. Add to the skillet and cook for 5 minutes. Add the cream and tomato sauce; cook for 10 minutes, or until reduced to one-third.

Cook the fettuccine in a large pot of boiling salted water according to the package directions, until just tender to the bite. Drain and add to the skillet. Stir to coat with the sauce. Sprinkle with the cheese and parsley.

LAVENDER HERB-MARINATED EGGPLANT

What can you do with eggplant when your garden is overflowing with this purple pleasure? Fry up a batch of this lavender-scented side dish.

MAKES 4 TO 6 SERVINGS

1½ pounds eggplant
Sea salt
2 cups extra-virgin olive oil
½ cup all-purpose flour
¼ cup chopped roasted red bell
    pepper
1 serrano chile pepper, minced
1 garlic clove, minced
1 tablespoon dried culinary
    'Provence' lavender buds, finely
    ground in a spice grinder
1 teaspoon lemon thyme or
    thyme leaves
1 teaspoon minced chives
1 teaspoon minced fresh Italian
    parsley leaves
1 teaspoon minced fresh mint leaves
Freshly ground black pepper

Cut the eggplant lengthwise into ⅛-inch-thick slices. Sprinkle generously with salt and place on a baking sheet to drain for 30 minutes. Rinse with cold water and pat dry with paper towels.

Place 1⅔ cups of the oil in a large heavy skillet. Warm over high heat until the surface just starts to shimmer but not smoke. Place the flour on a large plate. Working in batches, dip the eggplant into the flour to coat both sides and shake off any excess. Fry the slices until browned on both sides. Transfer to a baking sheet lined with paper towels. Let cool.

In a blender, combine the bell pepper, chile pepper, garlic, lavender, thyme, chives, parsley, mint, and the remaining ⅓ cup oil. Blend until smooth and creamy. Season with salt and pepper.

Layer a few eggplant slices in a deep serving dish. Spoon some of the herb marinade over the eggplant. Repeat until all the eggplant and marinade have been used. Refrigerate for 6 hours or overnight. Return to room temperature before serving.

Stuffed Peppers with Lavender Couscous
and Artichokes

Turn brightly colored peppers into little bowls holding artichokes, olives, and other flavorful ingredients. They'll really dress up your menu with warm summer colors and a taste of the Mediterranean.

Bocconcini are small mozzarella balls, about an inch in diameter. Pearl mozzarella balls are even smaller—about the size of pearls. They're available in many upscale grocery markets.

MAKES 8 SERVINGS

1 cup uncooked couscous
2 tablespoons unsalted butter
1 cup chicken broth
2 teaspoons dried culinary
    'Provence' lavender buds, finely
    ground in a spice grinder
3 tablespoons plus 1 teaspoon
    extra-virgin olive oil
1 (10-ounce) package frozen
    artichoke hearts, thawed,
    trimmed of rough edges,
    and quartered
2 shallots, chopped
4 ounces prosciutto, finely chopped
½ cup Niçoise olives, cut in half
    and pitted
½ cup pine nuts, toasted
¾ cup grated Parmesan cheese
Sea salt and freshly ground black
    pepper
2 red bell peppers
2 yellow bell peppers
½ pound fresh bocconcini
    mozzarella balls, cut in half,
    or pearl mozzarella balls

Place the couscous in a heatproof bowl and top with the butter. Bring the broth and lavender to a boil in a small saucepan and pour over the couscous. Stir, cover the bowl with foil, and set aside for 10 minutes. Fluff with a fork and set aside.

Heat 3 tablespoons of the oil in a large skillet over medium heat. Add the artichokes and shallots. Sauté for 10 minutes, or until the artichokes are soft and slightly browned. Stir into the couscous and let cool slightly. Add the prosciutto, olives, pine nuts, and half of the Parmesan. Stir well and season with salt and pepper.

Preheat the oven to 400°F. Slice the bell peppers in half lengthwise and remove the seeds and membranes. Brush the outside of the peppers with the remaining 1 teaspoon oil. Evenly divide the couscous mixture among the peppers. Place in a 13 x 9-inch baking dish, evenly distribute the mozzarella over the peppers, and sprinkle with the remaining Parmesan.

Pour about ½ inch of water into the bottom of the baking dish and cover the dish loosely with foil. Bake for 40 minutes, or until the peppers are very tender. Cool slightly before serving.

LAVENDER LEMON COOKIES

Celebrate any occasion with these lively lemon and lavender cookies. They're equally welcome at casual get-togethers and formal tea parties. You can make them a day ahead and store in an airtight container at room temperature. They're great served with black lavender tea.

Just before baking, they're sprinkled with lavender sugar. You can use regular granulated sugar, but large-crystal decorating sugar will really dress them up and give them sparkle. Look for it in gourmet stores and cake decorating shops. You might find it labeled sprinkling sugar or sanding sugar.

MAKES ABOUT 50 COOKIES

1 tablespoon dried culinary 'Provence' lavender buds
1 tablespoon plus ¾ cup sugar
¼ pound (1 stick) unsalted butter, at room temperature
1 large egg
1¼ teaspoons grated lemon zest
½ teaspoon vanilla extract
1¼ cups all-purpose flour
1½ teaspoons baking powder
¼ teaspoon salt
Lavender Lemon Syrup (recipe follows)
Lavender Sprinkling Sugar (recipe follows)

Combine the lavender and 1 tablespoon of the sugar in a spice grinder and pulse until finely ground. Transfer to a large bowl. Add the butter and the remaining ¾ cup sugar. Beat with an electric mixer until smooth. Beat in the egg, lemon zest, and vanilla.

Sift together the flour, baking powder, and salt. Add to the butter mixture and beat until blended. Cover the bowl with plastic wrap and refrigerate for 3 hours or overnight, until the dough is well chilled.

On a lightly floured surface, roll the dough into 2 long logs (1 inch thick). Wrap in plastic and refrigerate for at least 1 hour to firm up the dough for slicing.

Prepare the syrup.

Prepare the sprinkling sugar.

Preheat the oven to 325°F. Line 2 baking sheets with parchment paper.

Slice the logs into ½-inch coins and place on the prepared baking sheets. Using a pastry brush, generously coat the top side of the cookies with the syrup. Dust with the sprinkling sugar. Bake for 8 to 12 minutes, or until golden brown. Transfer the cookies to a wire rack and cool completely.

Lavender Lemon Syrup

1 tablespoon dried culinary
   'Provence' lavender buds
1 tablespoon plus ¾ cup sugar
¾ cup fresh lemon juice, strained
1 tablespoon light corn syrup
   or honey
1 tablespoon grated lemon zest

Combine the lavender and 1 tablespoon of the sugar in a spice grinder and pulse until finely ground. Transfer to a small saucepan. Stir in the lemon juice, corn syrup or honey, lemon zest, and the remaining ¾ cup sugar.

Bring to a simmer over medium heat, stirring occasionally. Cook for 1 minute, or until the sugar is dissolved. Set aside to cool. If not using immediately, transfer to a jar with a tight-fitting lid and refrigerate for up to 1 week.

Lavender Sprinkling Sugar

½ teaspoon dried culinary
   'Provence' lavender buds
½ cup granulated sugar or
   large-crystal sparkling sugar

Combine the lavender and 1 tablespoon of the sugar in a spice grinder and pulse until finely ground. Transfer to a small bowl and stir in the remaining sugar. If not using immediately, transfer to a small jar with a tight-fitting lid and store at room temperature.

Lavender Raspberry and Blackberry Cream Tart

This glorious tart looks as though it came from an exclusive French patisserie, but it's a snap to make—
thanks to a no-cook filling and a crust that requires no rolling. I won't tell if you won't.
Serve the tart with the glorious berries showing or cloak them with a dusting of confectioners' sugar.

MAKES 10 TO 12 SERVINGS

No-Roll Tart Dough
   (recipe follows)
⅓ **cup raspberry preserves, heated**
   and strained
I **(8-ounce) container mascarpone**
   cheese
¼ **cup heavy cream**
⅓ **cup confectioners' sugar**
I **teaspoon grated orange zest**
I **teaspoon vanilla extract**
2 **cups fresh blackberries**
I **cup fresh raspberries**

Prepare the dough and refrigerate for at least 30 minutes.

Preheat the oven to 375°F.

Press the dough into a 9-inch tart pan with a removable bottom. Trim the edges and prick the bottom all over with a fork. Bake for 20 minutes, or until golden brown. Brush the bottom and sides of the crust with the preserves and bake for an additional 5 minutes. Transfer to a wire rack to cool.

In a large bowl, combine the mascarpone, cream, sugar, orange zest, and vanilla. Beat with an electric mixer until soft peaks form when you lift the beaters. Spread evenly in the cooled crust. Refrigerate until firm, at least 2 hours or up to I day.

Arrange the blackberries and raspberries in concentric circles atop the filling.

No-Roll Tart Dough

I½ **cups all-purpose flour**
I **cup walnuts**
3 **tablespoons sugar**
2 **tablespoons dried culinary**
   'Provence' lavender buds
¼ **teaspoon salt**
¼ **pound (I stick) cold unsalted**
   butter, cut into small pieces
I **large egg yolk**
2 **tablespoons ice water**

In the bowl of a food processor, combine the flour, walnuts, sugar, lavender, and salt. Pulse until the walnuts are finely ground. Scatter the butter over the mixture and pulse until the mixture resembles coarse crumbs.

In a cup, beat the egg yolk and water with a fork to combine. Add to the food processor and pulse to combine. Gather the dough and press into a flat, round disk. Wrap the dough in plastic wrap and refrigerate for at least 30 minutes.

Lavender Coconut Panna Cotta

with Raspberry Caramel Sauce

Cool, rich, and velvety on the palate, this Italian custard is deceptively easy to prepare. Dressed up with a fruity caramel sauce and toasted coconut, it's sure to impress.

MAKES 8 SERVINGS

¼ cup cold water
1 envelope unflavored gelatin
1½ cups unsweetened coconut milk
1½ cups heavy cream
1 cup sugar
1½ teaspoons dried culinary 'Provence' lavender buds, finely ground in a spice grinder
¼ cup sweet white wine, such as Moscato
1½ teaspoons vanilla extract
Raspberry Caramel Sauce (recipe follows)
1 pint assorted summer berries, such as raspberries, blueberries, and golden raspberries (garnish)
1 cup grated fresh coconut (garnish)

Place the water in a small saucepan and sprinkle with the gelatin. Let stand for 1 minute to soften. Stir over low heat for 1 to 2 minutes, or until the water is warm and the gelatin is dissolved. Remove from the heat.

In a medium saucepan, mix the coconut milk, cream, sugar, and lavender. Stir over medium heat for 3 minutes, or until the sugar dissolves. Remove from the heat and stir in the wine, vanilla, and gelatin.

Butter eight 6-ounce ramekins. Pour in the cream mixture. Cover with plastic wrap and refrigerate until set, at least 6 hours or up to 1 day.

Prepare the caramel sauce. Spoon the sauce onto individual dessert plates. Unmold the ramekins onto the plates. Garnish with the berries and coconut.

Raspberry Caramel Sauce

¼ pound (1 stick) unsalted butter
¼ cup water
2 tablespoons raspberry syrup (see note)
¾ cup sugar
2 cups heavy cream
½ teaspoon dried culinary 'Provence' lavender buds, finely ground in a spice grinder
½ teaspoon vanilla extract

In a medium saucepan, combine the butter, water, and raspberry syrup. Cook over medium heat until the butter is melted. Add the sugar and increase the heat to medium-high. Gently swirling the pan, bring to a boil without stirring and cook until golden caramel in color, about 10 minutes.

Remove from the heat. Stir in the cream, lavender, and vanilla. Simmer over medium heat, stirring, until smooth. Simmer for 5 minutes more. Let cool.

Raspberry syrup can be found in the syrup section of the supermarket, next to the maple syrup.

Lavender Macadamia Nut Cookies

When I was in Australia visiting a lavender farm, I came up with the idea of adding lavender to a cookie recipe given to me by my good friend Carmen Jones. You'll love these sweet bites as much as the staff at Mon Chéri Cooking School does. Store the cookies in an airtight container at room temperature for up to 3 days. Or place in heavy-duty plastic bags and freeze for up to 90 days.

MAKES ABOUT 72 COOKIES

1 tablespoon dried culinary 'Provence' lavender buds

2 cups granulated sugar

1 pound (4 sticks) unsalted butter, at room temperature

½ cup packed dark brown sugar

2 large eggs

2 tablespoons vanilla extract

1½ teaspoons salt

5 cups all-purpose flour

1½ teaspoons baking soda

2½ cups sweetened shredded coconut

3½ cups coarsely chopped macadamia nuts

Preheat the oven to 350°F. Grease baking sheets or line with parchment paper.

Combine the lavender and 1 tablespoon of the granulated sugar in a spice grinder and pulse until finely ground. Stir into the remaining granulated sugar.

Place the butter in a large bowl and beat with an electric mixer until fluffy. Add the granulated sugar and brown sugar. Beat for 3 to 4 minutes, until very light. Beat in 1 egg at a time until incorporated. Beat in the vanilla and salt.

In another large bowl, mix the flour and baking soda. With the mixer on low speed, gradually add the flour to the butter mixture. When just incorporated, add the coconut and mix briefly. Stir in the nuts by hand. Cover and refrigerate for 2 hours.

Drop the dough by rounded tablespoons, 2 to 3 inches apart, on the prepared baking sheets. Flatten the cookies slightly with fork tines or your fingers. Bake for 10 to 13 minutes, or until the cookies are lightly browned at the edges and look set (but not browned) on top. Cool on a wire rack.

Very Lavender Apricot Cake
with Mascarpone Lavender Frosting

I had a vision of a beautiful layer cake, fragrant with lavender and apricots. It took us a while to develop the recipe to match my dream . . . but it was well worth the time. Thankfully, my friend food chemist and cookbook author Shirley Corriher helped us with a simple change.

MAKES 8 TO 12 SERVINGS

1 cup dried apricot halves

2 cups sugar

3 cups all-purpose flour

2 teaspoons baking powder

1 teaspoon baking soda

½ teaspoon salt

½ pound (2 sticks) unsalted butter,
    at room temperature

4 teaspoons dried 'Provence'
    lavender, finely ground in
    a spice grinder

Grated zest of 1 orange

Grated zest of 1 lemon

1½ teaspoons vanilla extract

4 large eggs

1 cup plain yogurt

Mascarpone Lavender Frosting
    (recipe follows)

1 cup dried apricots, finely
    chopped (garnish)

3 apricot roses (see note), garnish

Preheat the oven to 350°F. Grease two 8-inch cake pans or coat with nonstick spray. Line the bottoms with rounds of parchment paper and grease the paper. Flour the pans and tap out the excess.

In a food processor, combine the apricot halves and 1 cup of the sugar. Pulse for 30 seconds, or until the apricots are finely ground.

In a medium bowl, mix the flour, baking powder, baking soda, and salt.

Place the butter in a large bowl and beat with an electric mixer until fluffy. Slowly beat in the remaining 1 cup sugar, the apricot mixture, and then the lavender. Beat for 30 seconds. Beat in the orange zest, lemon zest, and vanilla.

One at a time, beat in the eggs, waiting for each to be incorporated before adding the next one. On low speed, add one-third of the flour mixture; when almost incorporated, add half of the yogurt. Repeat, then beat in the remaining flour. Scrape down the sides of the bowl and beat for another 5 to 10 seconds.

Divide between the prepared pans. Bake for 35 to 45 minutes, or until the tops are light golden brown and a toothpick inserted in the center comes out mostly clean, with just a few moist crumbs attached. Cool on a wire rack.

Prepare the frosting.

Run a sharp knife around the edge of each pan to detach the cake. Unmold onto a wire rack and peel off the parchment.

Place one layer, upside down, on a cake plate. Top with a layer of the frosting. Add the second layer, right side up. Frost the top and sides with the remaining frosting. Garnish the sides with the finely chopped apricots and place the apricot roses on top.

Mascarpone Lavender Frosting

4 tablespoons unsalted butter,
   at room temperature
1 (8-ounce) package cream cheese,
   at room temperature
8 ounces mascarpone cheese,
   at room temperature
2¼ cups confectioners' sugar, sifted
2 tablespoons apricot preserves
   or jam
1 teaspoon vanilla extract
1 teaspoon dried 'Provence'
   lavender, finely ground in
   a spice grinder

Place the butter in a large bowl and beat with an electric mixer until fluffy. Beat in the cream cheese and mascarpone. Turn off the mixer and add the confectioners' sugar, preserves or jam, vanilla, and lavender. Beat on low speed until the sugar is incorporated. Beat on medium high until the frosting is smooth and spreadable.

To make an apricot rose: Place 3 or 5 apricot halves between sheets of parchment paper and flatten with a meat pounder. Shape them into a rose by rolling 1 apricot into a cone shape and pressing the remaining apricots (sticky side in) around the cone to simulate petals.

Yo Yo's Filled with
Lavender Cranberry Buttercream

Yo Yo's are a favorite cookie in Australia, and this recipe came from a good friend there, Maureen McKeon. I added lavender to the filling and found it worked really well with the cranberries. Try serving these cookies with Lavender Coconut Panna Cotta with Raspberry Caramel Sauce (page 97).

MAKES ABOUT 40 COOKIES

¾ pound (3 sticks) unsalted
   butter, at room temperature
1 cup confectioners' sugar, sifted
2 teaspoons vanilla extract
3 cups all-purpose flour
⅔ cup English custard powder,
   such as Bird's
Lavender Cranberry Buttercream
   (recipe follows)
Confectioners' sugar (optional)

Preheat the oven to 350°F. Line 2 baking sheets with parchment paper.

In a large bowl, combine the butter, sugar, and vanilla. Beat with an electric mixer until fluffy. Sift together the flour and custard powder. Slowly beat into the butter mixture.

Roll the mixture into small balls and place, 1 inch apart, on the prepared baking sheets. Press down lightly on each ball with the back of a floured fork to flatten slightly.

Bake for 15 to 19 minutes, or until a light biscuit color. Cool on a wire rack.

Prepare the buttercream filling.

Spread or pipe the buttercream on the flat side of half of the cookies. Top with the remaining cookies to make sandwiches. Dust with confectioners' sugar (if using).

Bird's Custard Powder is available at upscale grocery stores and at Cost Plus World Market, a nationwide international product store.

LAVENDER CRANBERRY BUTTERCREAM

½ cup cranberry juice
¼ cup sweetened dried cranberries
¼ pound (1 stick) unsalted butter
1¾ cups confectioners' sugar, sifted
1 teaspoon vanilla extract
½ teaspoon dried culinary 'Provence' lavender buds, finely ground in a spice grinder

In a small saucepan, combine the juice and cranberries. Simmer over medium heat for 5 minutes, or until softened. Let cool and then chop finely.

In a large bowl, combine the butter, sugar, and vanilla. Beat with an electric mixer until light and creamy. Beat in the cranberries and lavender.

AUTUMN LAVENDER

Earthy and Flavorful

CONTENTS

Rosemary's Spiced Lavender Walnuts

My friend Rosemary Huza makes these spiced walnuts for gifts during the holidays. I've added lavender and rosemary (which intensifies the lavender flavor). You can easily make a batch—or several—ahead of time for parties. And definitely make enough to give as gifts for the holidays. Simply put into small cellophane bags and tie up with your prettiest holiday ribbon.

MAKES 3 CUPS

2 cups walnut halves

1½ cups sugar

½ cup water

I teaspoon ground cinnamon

½ teaspoon sea salt

I tablespoon dried culinary 'Provence' lavender buds, crushed with a mortar and pestle (see note)

I teaspoon fresh rosemary leaves, finely chopped

Preheat the oven to 350°F.

Butter a rimmed baking sheet and spread the walnuts in it. Bake for 5 minutes, stirring once, until lightly browned and fragrant. Set aside.

In a medium saucepan, combine the sugar, water, cinnamon, and salt. Over medium heat, boil without stirring until the mixture reads 238°F (soft-ball stage) on a candy thermometer. *Caution:* The sugar syrup is very hot. Remove from the heat and stir in the lavender, rosemary, and walnuts. Work quickly and stir gently until all the nuts are coated.

Transfer the nuts to the buttered baking sheet and spread them in an even layer, separating them with two buttered forks.

Cool. Store in an airtight container at room temperature or in a heavy plastic bag in the freezer.

By crushing the lavender with a mortar and pestle instead of a spice grinder, you can release the essential oils and still keep the buds partially intact. This gives the nuts more visual appeal, because you can see the bits of lavender flowers in the sugar coating.

Southwest Lavender Artichoke Frittata Bites

The spicy flavors we associate with the Southwest have been joined by lavender. Huge farms are now growing lavender in this part of the country, and an intriguing new flavor has developed.

This Italian egg dish is easy to prepare and can be cut into a generous amount of appetizers. Store some in the freezer for last-minute entertaining.

MAKES 56 SERVINGS

2 (8-ounce) packages frozen artichoke hearts, thawed and coarsely chopped

2 tablespoons extra-virgin olive oil

2 small red onions, finely chopped

4 garlic cloves, minced

¼ cup chopped canned green chile peppers

¼ cup oil-packed sun-dried tomatoes, blotted of excess oil and chopped

8 large eggs

½ cup fine dry bread crumbs

2 teaspoons dried culinary 'Provence' lavender buds, finely ground in a spice grinder

½ teaspoon sea salt

¼ teaspoon freshly ground black pepper

¼ teaspoon dried oregano

¼ teaspoon hot-pepper sauce

4 cups shredded sharp Cheddar cheese

¼ cup fresh Italian parsley leaves, minced

Preheat the oven to 325°F. Line a 13 x 9-inch baking dish with parchment paper.

In a large skillet over medium heat, sauté the artichokes in the oil for about 5 minutes. Add the onions and garlic. Cook, stirring, for 5 minutes, or until the onions are soft. Stir in the chile peppers and tomatoes.

Place the eggs in a large bowl and beat with a fork to combine. Stir in the bread crumbs, lavender, salt, black pepper, oregano, and pepper sauce. Stir in the cheese, parsley, and artichoke mixture. Pour into the prepared pan and spread evenly.

Bake for 30 minutes, or until the top is firm when lightly touched. Cut into small squares and serve hot, at room temperature, or cold. (To reheat, bake uncovered at 325°F for 10 to 12 minutes, or until hot.)

COUNTRY-STYLE LAVENDER TERRINE

Here's something rustic looking yet special for a party. You can make the terrine up to 3 days ahead (or a month if you freeze it), so there's no last-minute fuss. To be sure the uncooked mixture is perfectly seasoned, form a small spoonful of it into a patty, sauté, and taste. Adjust the seasonings as needed.

MAKES 40 SERVINGS

2 medium white onions, finely chopped

2 tablespoons unsalted butter

2 pounds ground veal

1 pound ground turkey

½ cup nonfat milk powder

4 large eggs

2 tablespoons dry white wine

1 tablespoon sea salt

2 teaspoons dried culinary 'Provence' lavender buds, finely ground in a spice grinder

1 teaspoon dried thyme

½ teaspoon ground ginger

½ teaspoon ground cloves

½ teaspoon freshly ground black pepper

4 garlic cloves, minced

18 prosciutto slices

1 (8-ounce) jar cornichon pickles

2 French baguettes, sliced ¼ inch thick

Dijon mustard

Preheat the oven to 350°F.

In a large skillet over medium heat, sauté the onions in the butter for 5 minutes, or until tender. Transfer to a large bowl and let cool for 10 minutes. Add the veal, turkey, milk powder, eggs, wine, salt, lavender, thyme, ginger, cloves, pepper, and garlic. Mix well.

Line a 10-inch springform pan with a circle of parchment paper. Line with about 14 slices of the prosciutto, allowing the ends to come up the sides of the pan. Add the meat mixture and press firmly and evenly into the pan. Cover with the remaining prosciutto; fold the loose ends over the top all around to make an attractive pattern.

Cover with another circle of parchment paper. Wrap the entire springform pan with heavy-duty foil to make the pan watertight. Place in a roasting pan and add enough hot water to come halfway up the sides of the springform pan.

Bake for 1½ hours. Remove from the oven. Let cool for 10 minutes. Remove the foil and carefully pour off any excess liquid. Press a piece of heavy-duty foil onto the top surface of the meat. Top with a flat plate about the same diameter as the pan.

Wrap clean bricks in heavy-duty foil (or use heavy cans) and place them evenly over the surface to help compress the meat mixture. Refrigerate overnight.

Unmold on a serving platter and cut into ¼-inch wedges. Serve at room temperature with the cornichons, baguette slices, and mustard.

GRANDMA'S LAVENDER POTATO ROLLS

I've added lavender to my grandmother's wonderful old recipe for potato dinner rolls. Serve warm, expect raves!

MAKES ABOUT 24 ROLLS

1 large russet potato, peeled and
    cubed
¼ cup warm water (about 110° to
    115°F)
1 package active dried yeast
1 cup milk, heated to 180°F and
    cooled to lukewarm
4 tablespoons unsalted butter,
    at room temperature
1 large egg
½ teaspoon sea salt
1 cup finely diced or shredded
    sharp white Cheddar cheese
¼ cup minced green onion
1 tablespoon finely chopped fresh
    lemon thyme or thyme
1 tablespoon dried culinary
    'Provence' lavender buds
4 cups all-purpose flour
1 large egg, slightly beaten (glaze)

Place the potato in a medium saucepan and cover generously with cold water. Bring to a boil over medium-high heat, then reduce the heat and simmer until tender, about 10 minutes. Drain and cool. Mash and measure out ½ cup for the rolls; reserve any remainder for another use.

Place the warm water in a large bowl and sprinkle with the yeast. Let stand for 5 minutes, or until foamy. Stir in the potatoes, milk, butter, salt, and 1 egg. Then stir in the cheese, green onion, and thyme.

Place the lavender and 1 teaspoon of the flour in a spice grinder. Pulse until finely ground. Add to the bowl. Stir in 2 cups of the flour. Stir in enough of the remaining flour to make a soft dough. Turn out onto a lightly floured surface and knead for 6 to 8 minutes, or until smooth and elastic.

Oil a large bowl, add the dough, and turn to coat the top. Cover and let rise in a warm place until doubled in size, about 1 hour. Punch down and shape into a ball. Cover and let rise for 10 minutes.

Grease 2 baking sheets. Pinch off small amounts of dough (about the size of a lime) and shape into rolls. Place on the baking sheets with at least ½ inch space between them. Let rise until almost doubled in size, about 1 hour.

Preheat the oven to 400°F. Glaze the rolls by brushing the surface with the slightly beaten egg. Bake for 10 to 12 minutes, or until golden brown.

Lavender Macadamia Pineapple Coffee Cake

A taste of the islands meets a taste of lavender in this crunchy, sweet, moist coffee cake. Include it in your next tea or brunch and no one will be able to resist!

MAKES 10 TO 12 SERVINGS

1 cup milk
1 tablespoon vinegar or lemon juice
2¼ cups all-purpose flour
2 teaspoons baking powder
½ teaspoon baking soda
½ teaspoon salt
1 tablespoon dried culinary
    'Provence' lavender buds, finely
    ground in a spice grinder
¼ pound (1 stick) unsalted butter,
    at room temperature
1 cup packed dark brown sugar
1 large egg
1 tablespoon orange liqueur
½ cup well-drained canned
    crushed pineapple
1½ cups coarsely chopped
    macadamia nuts
¼ cup heavy cream
1 large egg yolk
½ cup grated coconut
2 tablespoons granulated sugar
2 tablespoons grated orange zest

Preheat the oven to 350°F. Grease and flour a 9-inch cake pan.

Place the milk in a small saucepan and warm briefly over medium heat. Stir in the vinegar or lemon juice and set aside until the milk looks curdled.

Sift the flour, baking powder, baking soda, and salt into a medium bowl. Stir in the lavender.

Place the butter in a large bowl and beat with an electric mixer until fluffy. Beat in the brown sugar. Add the egg and continue beating, occasionally scraping down the sides of the bowl, for 5 minutes, or until fluffy.

Beginning with the dry ingredients, alternately beat in the flour and milk in three additions each. Beat in the liqueur and then the pineapple and ½ cup of the nuts. Pour into the prepared cake pan.

In a cup, mix the cream and egg yolk; pour over the batter.

In a small bowl, mix the coconut, granulated sugar, orange zest, and the remaining 1 cup nuts. Sprinkle over the batter.

Bake for 40 to 50 minutes, or until the center springs back when touched lightly. Let cool for 20 to 30 minutes before cutting.

Butterscotch Pumpkin Muffins
with Honey Lavender Butter

The comforting flavors of fall are baked into muffins that will have family and guests clamoring for another batch. Butterscotch chips add a flavor surprise that makes these treats even more irresistible.
Chop the crystallized ginger before you start mixing the batter. If it sticks to your knife, sprinkle with enough of the brown sugar to facilitate chopping.

MAKES 16 MUFFINS

Honey Lavender Butter
   (recipe follows)
1 cup unsweetened canned
   pumpkin puree
1 cup packed dark brown sugar
¼ pound (1 stick) unsalted butter,
   melted
2 large eggs
¼ cup apple cider
1¾ cups all-purpose flour
1 teaspoon baking powder
1 teaspoon baking soda
½ teaspoon salt
1 tablespoon dried culinary
   'Provence' lavender buds, finely
   ground in a spice grinder
1½ teaspoons ground ginger
½ teaspoon ground cinnamon
½ teaspoon grated nutmeg
¼ teaspoon ground cloves
¼ cup butterscotch chips
2 tablespoons finely chopped
   crystallized ginger
¼ cup pecans, chopped

Preheat the oven to 350°F. Place paper liners in 16 muffin cups (work in batches, if necessary).

Prepare the lavender butter.

In a large bowl, mix the pumpkin, brown sugar, and butter. Add the eggs and beat until smooth. Stir in the cider.

Sift the flour, baking powder, baking soda, salt, lavender, ground ginger, cinnamon, nutmeg, and cloves into a medium bowl. Gradually stir into the pumpkin mixture until thoroughly mixed. Fold in the butterscotch chips and crystallized ginger until evenly distributed.

Spoon the batter into the prepared muffin cups, filling each cup almost to the top. Sprinkle with the pecans.

Bake for 20 to 25 minutes, or until puffed and golden. Serve warm with the lavender butter.

HONEY LAVENDER BUTTER

¼ pound (1 stick) unsalted butter,
   at room temperature
1 tablespoon honey or lavender
   honey
1 tablespoon dried culinary
   'Provence' lavender buds, finely
   ground in a spice grinder

In the bowl of a food processor, combine the butter, honey, and lavender. Pulse until just mixed. Transfer to a sheet of parchment paper. Roll into a 1-inch-wide log. Refrigerate until ready to use.

HOT LAVENDER CRANBERRY PUNCH

When the weather turns nippy, this spiced punch goes down easy and warms you up. Serve in mugs with lemon or orange slices and a cinnamon stick stirrer. But don't forget about this drink come summer, because it's also great over ice.

MAKES 6 TO 8 SERVINGS

4 cups cranberry juice
1 cup orange juice
1 cup water
¼ cup sugar
2 tablespoons fresh lemon juice
½ small cinnamon stick
2 whole cloves
½ teaspoon dried culinary
   'Provence' lavender buds

In a large saucepan, combine the cranberry juice, orange juice, water, sugar, lemon juice, cinnamon, cloves, and lavender. Bring to a simmer over medium heat and cook for 5 minutes. Strain.

Lavender Hot Buttered Rum

Nothing tastes better on a cold autumn evening than hot buttered rum. And as good as the original is, this lavender version will really delight you.

You can store the butter mixture for up to 1 week in the refrigerator or up to 2 months in the freezer. Keep a batch on hand for unexpected guests.

MAKES 8 TO 10 SERVINGS

¼ pound (1 stick) unsalted butter,
    at room temperature
½ cup packed light brown sugar
½ teaspoon ground cinnamon
¼ teaspoon dried culinary
    'Provence' lavender buds, finely
    ground in a spice grinder
Pinch of ground allspice
Pinch of ground cloves
Pinch of grated nutmeg
Pinch of salt
Boiling water
Rum

In the bowl of a food processor, combine the butter, brown sugar, cinnamon, lavender, allspice, cloves, nutmeg, and salt. Process until the mixture turns into a light brown paste.

To serve, pour boiling water into coffee mugs, add a heaping tablespoon of the paste, and stir to dissolve. Add rum to taste.

LAVENDER MULLED WINE

Light up the fireplace, ladle out this mulled wine, and settle in for a cozy evening as the frost dusts the pumpkins. Serve in mugs garnished with lemon or orange slices and cinnamon sticks.

MAKES 8 SERVINGS

1 (750-milliliter) bottle dry red
   wine, such as a fruity Merlot
   (see note)

½ cup sugar

1 cinnamon stick

1 teaspoon dried culinary
   'Provence' lavender buds

6 allspice berries

2 whole cloves

2 (3-inch) strips of lemon zest

In a large saucepan, combine the wine, sugar, cinnamon, lavender, allspice, cloves, and lemon zest. Bring to a simmer over medium heat. Cook for about 5 minutes. Strain.

Be sure to choose a moderately priced wine. With the addition of sugar and spices, much of the subtlety of a more expensive wine will be lost.

Butternut Squash Bisque
with Lavender Cider Cream

Don't be surprised if this becomes one of your family's favorites. It's so full of delicious autumn flavors that you'll want to serve it over and over again.

MAKES 8 TO 10 SERVINGS

Lavender Cider Cream
    (recipe follows)
5 tablespoons unsalted butter
2 cups finely diced leek
½ cup finely diced carrot
½ cup finely diced celery
2½ pounds butternut squash,
    peeled, seeded, and cut
    into ½-inch cubes
2 small tart apples, peeled, cored,
    and diced
2 teaspoons dried culinary
    'Provence' lavender buds, finely
    ground in a spice grinder
1½ teaspoons fresh lemon thyme
    or thyme leaves
½ teaspoon chopped fresh
    marjoram leaves
6 cups chicken broth
½ cup frozen apple juice
    concentrate, thawed
1 bunch fresh chives, finely chopped

Prepare the cider cream.

Melt the butter in a large pot over medium heat. Add the leek, carrot, and celery. Sauté for 10 minutes, or until the leeks are translucent. Add the squash and sauté for 5 minutes. Stir in the apples, lavender, thyme, and marjoram. Stir in the broth and juice concentrate. Bring to a simmer.

Cover and simmer for 30 minutes, or until the squash and apples are very tender. Using a handheld blender or a food processor (work in batches), blend the soup until smooth. Return to a simmer.

Ladle into individual bowls. Swirl 1 to 2 tablespoons of the cider cream into each bowl. Sprinkle with the chives.

LAVENDER CIDER CREAM

¼ cup apple cider jelly (see note)

⅔ cup sour cream or crème fraîche (see note)

1 teaspoon dried culinary 'Provence' lavender buds, lightly ground with a mortar and pestle

Place the jelly in a small saucepan and stir over low heat just until melted. Remove from the heat and whisk in the sour cream or crème fraîche and lavender. Transfer to a small bowl and refrigerate until needed.

If apple cider jelly is not available, bring ½ cup of apple cider to a boil in a small saucepan and cook until reduced to ¼ cup. Let cool.

Crème fraîche is a rich, thickened cream with a slightly tangy flavor. Look for it in upscale supermarkets or make your own, with or without lavender (see page 21).

Taos Lavender Potato Soup

*This tasty soup underscores the word **flavor**! Full, robust flavors of chiles are softened with potatoes and cream to warm your cool autumn days.*
The recipe does make quite a large pot of soup. You can cut it in half if you want, but then you'll be sorry it's gone so soon!

MAKES 8 TO 10 SERVINGS

1 teaspoon cumin seeds
1½ tablespoons dried culinary 'Provence' lavender buds
¼ pound (1 stick) unsalted butter
6 leeks, cut in half lengthwise and thinly sliced (white and pale green parts only)
2 medium carrots, diced
1 celery rib with leaves, finely chopped
3 garlic cloves, chopped
3 tablespoons all-purpose flour
16 cups chicken broth
10 medium russet potatoes, peeled and thinly sliced
3 fresh medium poblano chile peppers, roasted, peeled, seeded, and chopped
2 teaspoons minced chipotle pepper in adobo sauce
1 tablespoon black peppercorns
4 bay leaves
2 cups heavy cream
Sea salt and freshly ground black pepper
6 green onions, chopped

Toast the cumin seeds in a dry skillet over medium heat until fragrant, about 2 minutes. Transfer to a spice grinder and add the lavender. Pulse until finely ground.

Melt the butter in a large pot over medium heat. Add the leeks, carrots, celery, and garlic. Cook for 5 minutes, or until the leeks are soft. Stir in the flour. Add the broth, potatoes, poblano peppers, chipotle pepper, and lavender mixture.

Tie up the peppercorns and bay leaves in a small square of cheesecloth. Add to the pot. Simmer for 25 minutes, or until the potatoes are tender. Remove and discard the cheesecloth bundle. Using a handheld blender or a food processor (work in batches), blend the soup until smooth. Stir in the cream. Season with salt and pepper. Ladle into individual soup bowls and sprinkle with the green onions.

Lavender Cream of Mushroom Soup
with Goat Cheese Croustades

Earthy mushrooms pair well with lavender in a soup that's rich, smooth, and satisfying. It's perfect for a light dinner, served with a simple salad. Although a touch of cream silkens the soup's texture, you may omit it if you're watching calories.

MAKES 8 SERVINGS

Lavender Goat Cheese Croustades
  (recipe follows)
2 tablespoons unsalted butter
3 leeks, cut in half lengthwise
  and thinly sliced (white and
  pale green parts only)
3 tablespoons finely chopped shallot
2 pounds small brown mushrooms,
  thinly sliced
1 teaspoon dried culinary
  'Provence' lavender buds, finely
  ground in a spice grinder
1 bay leaf
$\frac{1}{4}$ teaspoon chopped fresh lemon
  thyme or thyme leaves
2 garlic cloves, minced
Sea salt and freshly ground black
  pepper
$\frac{1}{4}$ cup uncooked long-grain
  white rice
2 tablespoons all-purpose flour
$3\frac{1}{4}$ cups reduced-sodium chicken
  broth
$3\frac{1}{4}$ cups beef broth
$\frac{1}{2}$ cup port wine
$\frac{1}{2}$ cup heavy cream
2 tablespoons fresh Italian parsley
  leaves, minced
$\frac{1}{4}$ cup chopped chives

Prepare the croustades.

Melt the butter in a large pot over medium heat. Add the leeks and shallot. Cook for 5 minutes, or until the leeks are soft. Add the mushrooms, lavender, bay leaf, thyme, and garlic. Season with salt and pepper. Cook for 10 minutes, or until most of the liquid released by the mushrooms has evaporated. Stir in the rice and flour. Cook for 2 minutes.

Add the chicken broth, beef broth, and port. Bring to a boil. Cover, reduce the heat to medium-low, and simmer for 20 minutes, stirring occasionally. Add the cream and simmer for 10 minutes, stirring occasionally. Correct the seasoning and remove the bay leaf.

Ladle into soup bowls and sprinkle with the parsley and chives. Serve with the croustades (if desired, float them in the bowls).

¼ cup extra-virgin olive oil
  (see note)
1 teaspoon minced garlic
1 French baguette, sliced ¼ inch
  thick
5 ounces soft goat cheese
1 tablespoon dried culinary
  'Provence' lavender buds, finely
  ground in a spice grinder

Preheat the oven to 400°F.

Combine the oil and garlic in a small saucepan and cook over medium heat for about 1 minute to infuse the oil with the garlic flavor. Brush the top side of each bread slice with the oil mixture and place in a single layer on a baking sheet.

Bake for 9 to 10 minutes, or until lightly browned. Remove from the oven and cool. If not using immediately, store in an airtight container.

To serve, mix the goat cheese and lavender. Spread on the croustades.

For great flavor, use oil left from Lavender-Marinated Goat Cheese (page 81).

Provençal Green Salad
with Lavender-Encrusted Baked Goat Cheese

This is a variation of a recipe from my friend Peggy Fallon, who taught an appetizer class at Mon Chéri Cooking School. Goat cheese slices become heavenly morsels when marinated in olive oil, rolled in lavender bread crumbs, and baked. Add croutons and Niçoise olives and you've got a perfect mix of cream and crunch. Use a nice mixture of greens, such as butter lettuce, radicchio, Belgian endive, and curly endive.

MAKES 6 TO 8 SERVINGS

Garlic Croustades (recipe follows)
1 (8-ounce) log goat cheese, cut
    into ½-inch slices
1 cup extra-virgin olive oil
1½ cups fresh bread crumbs
    (see note)
1½ tablespoons dried culinary
    'Provence' lavender buds, finely
    ground in a spice grinder
Lavender Balsamic Dressing
    (recipe follows)
8 cups lightly packed assorted
    fall greens
24 Niçoise olives

Prepare the croustades.

In a glass bowl or jar, combine the oil and goat cheese. Cover and refrigerate for at least 30 minutes or up to several days.

Preheat the oven to 400°F. Line a baking sheet with a piece of parchment paper.

Using a spoon or fork, transfer the goat cheese from the oil to a colander set over a bowl. Let drain for a few minutes (reserve the oil and use for the dressing).

On a plate, mix the bread crumbs and lavender. Roll the cold cheese slices in the crumbs to coat all over. Place the slices on the prepared baking sheet and bake for 5 to 10 minutes, or until they're lightly browned but still keep their shape.

While the cheese bakes, prepare the dressing.

Place the greens in a large bowl and toss with the dressing. Divide among individual plates. Top with the warm goat cheese and garnish with the croustades and olives. Serve immediately.

 It's easy to make fresh bread crumbs—and it's a good way to use up stale bread. Simply tear the slices into big pieces and finely grind them in a food processor.

GARLIC CROUSTADES

1 French baguette, sliced ¼ inch
thick
Extra-virgin olive oil
1 garlic clove, cut in half

Preheat the oven to 400°F.

Brush the top side of each bread slice with oil and place in a single layer on a baking sheet. Bake for 9 to 10 minutes, or until lightly browned. Remove from the oven and rub with the cut side of the garlic. Cool. If not using immediately, store in an airtight container.

LAVENDER BALSAMIC DRESSING

½ cup extra-virgin olive oil
(see note)
2 tablespoons red wine vinegar
2 tablespoons balsamic vinegar
1 teaspoon honey mustard
1 teaspoon dried culinary
'Provence' lavender buds, finely
ground in a spice grinder
1 garlic clove, finely minced
Sea salt and freshly ground black
pepper

In a small bowl, whisk together the oil, wine vinegar, balsamic vinegar, mustard, lavender, and garlic. Season with salt and pepper. Cover and refrigerate until needed.

For more flavor, use the drained oil from the marinated goat cheese.

Avocados and Pears

with Raspberry Lavender Vinaigrette

Avocados and pears have a natural affinity. The raspberry vinaigrette provides an elegant counterpoint to their delicate nature. Be careful not to cut the avocado more than half an hour in advance or it will discolor. And be aware that if you prepare the dressing more than a few hours ahead, you'll lose its lovely pink color.

MAKES 4 TO 6 SERVINGS

Lavender Poached Pears
 (recipe follows)
Raspberry Lavender Vinaigrette
 (recipe follows)
**2 avocados, halved, pitted, and
 peeled**
3 tablespoons extra-virgin olive oil
2 cups mixed greens
½ pint fresh raspberries
**2 tablespoons edible flower petals
 (garnish, see note)**

Prepare the pears.

Prepare the vinaigrette.

Place the avocado halves on a cutting board, rounded side up. Slice lengthwise and fan out the slices. Do the same with the pears. Brush all the slices with the oil.

Spread the greens on a large platter. Arrange the avocados and pears over the greens, alternating them to make a design. Top with the dressing and raspberries. Garnish with the flowers.

Some upscale supermarkets sell edible flowers in their produce section. Nasturtiums and pansies work great in this recipe. Be aware that although many flowers are deliciously edible, not all are. So be sure you know that your chosen ones are meant to be eaten before serving them.

Lavender Poached Pears

2 pears, preferably Anjou or Bosc
3 cups water
½ cup sugar
¼ cup fresh lemon juice
**1 tablespoon dried culinary
 'Provence' lavender buds, finely
 ground in a spice grinder**

Peel, quarter, and core the pears. Place in a medium saucepan. Add the water, sugar, lemon juice, and lavender. Bring to a simmer over medium heat and cook for 15 to 20 minutes, or until the pears are tender when you pierce them with a skewer or sharp knife. Remove from the heat and allow the pears to cool in the liquid.

RASPBERRY LAVENDER VINAIGRETTE

1 cup fresh raspberries
1 teaspoon fresh lemon juice
2 teaspoons dried culinary
    'Provence' lavender buds, finely
    ground in a spice grinder
Pinch of sugar
1/3 cup extra-virgin olive oil
Sea salt and freshly ground black
    pepper

In the bowl of a food processor, combine the raspberries, lemon juice, lavender, and sugar. With the machine running, slowly add the oil. Season with salt and pepper. If needed, adjust the seasoning with more sugar or lemon juice.

CANTALOUPE, MANGO, AND ASIAN PEAR SALAD
WITH LAVENDER CILANTRO DRESSING

You'll love the balance of soft and crunchy textures contributed by the Asian pear, melon, jicama, and mango. Lavender's magical presence in the dressing ties them all together.

MAKES 4 SERVINGS

Lavender Cilantro Dressing
    (recipe follows)
1 large cantaloupe, seeded, peeled,
    and cubed
1 mango, peeled, seeded, and cubed
1 Asian pear, peeled, cored,
    and cubed
1 red bell pepper, diced
1 small jicama, peeled and diced
1/2 medium red onion, cut into
    1/8-inch slivers (see note)
1 head romaine lettuce
2 starfruit, thinly sliced

Prepare the dressing.

In a large bowl, combine the cantaloupe, mango, pear, pepper, jicama, and onion. Add half of the dressing and toss to coat. Cover and refrigerate for at least 1 hour or up to 4 hours.

Line a serving platter with the lettuce leaves. Mound the salad on top and drizzle with the remaining dressing. Scatter the starfruit around the platter.

To make onion slivers, first cut the onion into quarters lengthwise (from sprout to root end). Then slice thinly in the same direction.

Lavender Cilantro Dressing

¾ cup orange juice

2 tablespoons fresh lemon juice

2 tablespoons fresh lime juice

I teaspoon cumin seeds

I teaspoon dried culinary
   'Provence' lavender buds

½ cup lightly packed fresh
   cilantro leaves

2 tablespoons lavender honey
   or orange honey

1½ teaspoons minced chipotle
   pepper in adobo sauce

I teaspoon grated orange zest

¼ cup extra-virgin olive oil

Sea salt and freshly ground black
   pepper

In a small saucepan, combine the orange juice, lemon juice, and lime juice. Bring to a boil over medium heat and cook until reduced to ½ cup. Let cool for 10 minutes, then transfer to a blender.

Toast the cumin seeds in a small skillet over medium-high heat for 2 minutes, or until fragrant. Transfer to a spice grinder and add the lavender. Pulse until finely ground. Add to the blender.

Add the cilantro, honey, chipotle pepper, and orange zest. Pulse until smooth. Add the oil and blend until smooth and creamy. Season with salt and pepper.

Apricot-Lavender Chicken
on a Bed of Apples, Dried Apricots, and Pecans

President Clinton and his entourage enjoyed this grilled chicken dish while visiting Silicon Valley in 1993. Enhanced with a hint of bourbon and orange zest, the chicken makes an ideal entrée for a wedding buffet or an elegant luncheon. Served on a bed of fruit and nuts, this dish bursts with the flavors and colors of the fall season.

MAKES 8 SERVINGS

Chicken
2 (11½-ounce) cans apricot nectar
1 cup apricot preserves
¼ cup lavender vinegar or white
    wine vinegar
¼ cup honey mustard
¼ cup bourbon
2 tablespoons dried culinary
    'Provence' lavender buds, finely
    ground in a spice grinder
1 tablespoon coarse sea salt
8 boneless, skinless chicken
    breast halves

Fruit
½ cup pineapple juice
4 apples (see note)
¾ cup toasted pecans
¼ cup dried apricots, julienned
2 tablespoons julienned orange zest
1 tablespoon dried culinary
    'Provence' lavender buds,
    crushed with a mortar and pestle
1 apricot rose (garnish, see note)

To make the chicken: In a large bowl, mix the apricot nectar, preserves, vinegar, mustard, bourbon, lavender, and salt. Transfer ½ cup to a small bowl, cover, and refrigerate until needed.

If necessary, remove the tenderloin pieces from the chicken and reserve for another use. Add the chicken to the remaining marinade and turn to coat all sides. Cover and refrigerate overnight.

Preheat a gas grill to medium.

Drain the chicken and discard the marinade. Place the chicken on the grill, skin side down. Cook, basting occasionally with the reserved ½ cup marinade, for 25 to 30 minutes, or until the chicken is no longer pink when tested with a sharp knife.

Transfer to a clean plate and refrigerate for at least 1 hour. Slice crosswise into thin pieces, keeping the breasts together.

To make the fruit: Place the pineapple juice in a large bowl. Cut the apples into julienne (matchstick) pieces with a knife or a mandoline; as you work, add them to the bowl and toss to coat with the juice. Drain off the juice. Add the pecans, apricots, and orange zest. Toss to combine and transfer to a platter. Sprinkle with the lavender.

Arrange the chicken on top, fanning out the pieces. Garnish with the apricot rose.

I like to use Fuji, Granny Smith, or McIntosh apples for this dish. Soaking the cut apples in pineapple juice keeps them from turning brown without significantly affecting their flavor.

To make an apricot rose: Place 3 or 5 apricots between sheets of parchment paper and flatten with a meat pounder. Shape them into a rose by rolling 1 apricot into a cone shape and pressing the remaining apricots (sticky side in) around the cone to simulate petals.

Breakfast Corn Crêpes
Filled with Scrambled Eggs and Apple Sausage

Plan a day out with family or friends enjoying the beauty of autumn. But before you go, consider a special hearty breakfast or brunch. Serve these crêpes with hot cider, coffee, orange juice, and sliced melon with grapes. This is a variation of a recipe from my good friend Marilyn Harris, who has a radio cooking show in Cincinnati.

If you want to get a head start on breakfast or brunch, assemble the crêpes the night before and refrigerate until needed. Bake at 350°F for 20 to 30 minutes, or until heated through.

MAKES 12 TO 18 CRÊPES

Lavender Corn Crêpes
(recipe follows)
Creamy Lavender Cheddar Sauce
(recipe follows)
Scrambled Eggs and Apple Sausage
(recipe follows)
¼ cup grated Parmesan cheese
1 avocado, halved, pitted, peeled,
and sliced (garnish)
Fresh Italian parsley sprigs
(garnish)

Prepare the crêpes.

Prepare the sauce.

Prepare the eggs and sausage.

Preheat the oven to 350°F. Butter a shallow casserole dish large enough to hold the filled crêpes in a single layer.

Fill each crêpe with 2 tablespoons of the egg mixture and roll up like a burrito (fold in the sides, then roll to enclose the filling). Place, seam side down, in the casserole dish.

Spoon the sauce over the crêpes and sprinkle with the cheese. Bake for 10 to 15 minutes. Serve garnished with the avocado and parsley.

Lavender Corn Crêpes

1 cup frozen corn kernels (see note)

3 large eggs

¾ cup milk

½ cup instant flour, such as Wondra

⅓ cup cornmeal

1 tablespoon dried culinary 'Provence' lavender buds, finely ground in a spice grinder

¾ teaspoon sea salt

1 teaspoon hot-pepper sauce

½ teaspoon dried thyme

6 tablespoons unsalted butter, melted

3 tablespoons finely minced chives

¼ cup vegetable oil

In a blender, combine the corn, eggs, milk, flour, cornmeal, lavender, salt, pepper sauce, thyme, and 2 tablespoons of the butter. Blend until smooth, stopping to scrape down the sides of the container as necessary. Pour into a bowl and stir in the chives. Cover and refrigerate for at least 1 hour.

Mix the oil and the remaining 4 tablespoons butter. Lightly brush a 7- or 8-inch crêpe pan with some of the mixture. Place over medium heat until hot.

Pour in about ¼ cup of the batter and swirl to evenly coat the bottom of the pan. If there's too much batter, pour out the excess; if there's not enough for even coverage, add a little more.

Cook for about 1 minute, or until lightly browned on the bottom and dry on top. Flip and cook for about 10 seconds, until slightly mottled on the bottom. Transfer to a wire rack and let cool. Repeat, brushing the pan with more oil mixture as needed. Stack the cooled crêpes as you work. If not using immediately, wrap tightly in plastic wrap and refrigerate.

When making this crêpe batter, don't thaw the corn before making the batter. Frozen corn grinds up much finer and easier.

CREAMY LAVENDER CHEDDAR SAUCE

2 cups milk
Pinch of dried culinary 'Provence' lavender buds
1 bay leaf
2 fresh Italian parsley sprigs
2 fresh thyme sprigs or a generous pinch of dried thyme
1/8 teaspoon grated nutmeg
1 small onion, cut into quarters
4 tablespoons unsalted butter
1/4 cup all-purpose flour
1/2 teaspoon sea salt
Dash of hot-pepper sauce
1/2 cup grated sharp white Cheddar cheese

In a small saucepan, combine the milk, lavender, bay leaf, parsley, thyme, nutmeg, and onion. Bring just to the boiling point over medium heat. Remove from the heat and let stand for at least 15 minutes. Strain and reheat.

Melt the butter in a medium saucepan over medium heat. Whisk in the flour. Cook, stirring, for at least 2 minutes; do not let the flour brown. Whisk in the warm milk, salt, and pepper sauce. Stir for 2 minutes, or until thickened and boiling. Remove from the heat and stir in the cheese until melted. Cover and keep warm.

SCRAMBLED EGGS AND APPLE SAUSAGE

1 pound cooked apple sausage links, sliced 1/4 inch thick
5 tablespoons unsalted butter
1/4 cup finely diced red bell pepper
1/4 cup finely diced yellow bell pepper
1/4 cup finely diced red onion
12 large eggs
1 tablespoon coarse-grained brown mustard
1 tablespoon dried culinary 'Provence' lavender buds, finely ground in a spice grinder
1/2 teaspoon sea salt
1/2 teaspoon freshly ground black pepper

In a large nonstick skillet over medium heat, sauté the sausage for 5 minutes, or until browned. Drain on paper towels and set aside.

Pour off the drippings and wipe out the skillet. Add the butter and allow to melt. Add the red pepper, yellow pepper, and onion. Sauté for 5 minutes, or until soft. Reduce the heat to low. Add the sausage.

In a large bowl, whisk together the eggs, mustard, lavender, salt, and pepper. Pour into the skillet and stir gently for 4 minutes, or until softly set and creamy. Remove from the skillet, place in a medium bowl, and cover to keep warm. The scrambled eggs will continue to cook after being removed from the pan.

When scrambling eggs, use low, gentle heat. If cooked at a high temperature, the eggs will toughen.

Mon Chéri Spinach-Stuffed Beef Tenderloin
with Lavender Port Sauce

I developed this dish several years ago, and it has become a favorite with my catering clients. It's great for a holiday, but it's easy enough for Sunday dinner! Serve the meat hot with the warm port sauce. Or chill and serve with crumbled blue cheese.

MAKES 8 SERVINGS

Spinach Filling

2 pounds fresh spinach
¼ cup extra-virgin olive oil
1 tablespoon dried culinary 'Provence' lavender buds, finely ground in a spice grinder
1 tablespoon minced garlic
½ cup pine nuts, toasted
½ cup grated Parmesan cheese
¼ cup chopped fresh basil leaves or prepared pesto

Beef

1 (5- to 6-pound) beef tenderloin
½ cup port wine
Sea salt and freshly ground white pepper
1 roasted red bell pepper, thinly sliced
Lavender Port Sauce (recipe follows)

To make the filling: Wash the spinach, remove tough stems, and pat dry. Roughly chop. Warm the oil in a large pot over medium heat. Stir in the lavender and garlic. Add the spinach and cook, stirring often, until the spinach wilts and all the moisture has evaporated. Cool. Stir in the pine nuts, cheese, and basil or pesto.

To make the beef: Preheat the oven to 350°F.

Remove any fat from the surface of the beef. Butterfly the beef (meaning turn the round loin into a big, long, rectangular, ¼-inch-thick slice of meat): Starting at one end, slice into the loin at an angle and make a cut down the length of the loin no more than ¼ inch thick. From this cut, start slicing into the loin, exactly parallel to the outer surface of the loin; work from one end of the loin to the other, always keeping a thickness of about ¼ inch. Keep this process going until you reach the inside of the loin. Lay the beef flat on a work surface and pound it a little flatter for easier rolling. Sprinkle with ¼ cup of the port and season with salt and pepper.

Spread the stuffing over the tenderloin, leaving a 1-inch border. Place the red pepper strips down the middle of the filling. Roll the beef up lengthwise, exactly as you would a jelly roll. Place the seam side down when finished.

Tie the meat with kitchen twine at 1-inch intervals to secure. Sprinkle with the remaining ¼ cup of port and season with salt and pepper. Place in a large roasting pan.

Roast for 30 minutes, or until a meat thermometer inserted into the thickest part of the tenderloin registers 135°F. Remove the meat from the oven and let rest for 15 minutes before slicing.

Prepare the port sauce and serve with the beef.

You may replace the fresh spinach with 2 (10-ounce) packages of frozen chopped spinach. Thaw and squeeze out the excess liquid.

LAVENDER PORT SAUCE

1½ cups beef broth

1½ tablespoons unsalted butter

2 teaspoons dried culinary
'Provence' lavender buds, finely
ground in a spice grinder

⅓ cup port wine

1 tablespoon cornstarch

¼ cup finely diced mushrooms

To make the sauce: In a small saucepan, combine the broth, butter, and lavender. Place over medium heat until the butter melts.

In a cup, mix the wine and cornstarch. Stir into the broth. Cook, stirring, for 3 minutes, or until the sauce thickens. Stir in the mushrooms. Keep warm. If not using immediately, cover and refrigerate for up to 1 day; rewarm over medium-low heat.

BAKED SPICY PORK CHOPS WITH LAVENDER AND APPLE

Make this easy, full-flavored pork dish when you're short on time. It's perfect for the family on the go and reheats beautifully.

MAKES 6 SERVINGS

6 pork chops, ¾ inch thick

1 tablespoon Spiced Lavender
Seasoning (page 18)

2 tablespoons extra-virgin olive oil

2 tablespoons unsalted butter

3 Granny Smith apples, peeled,
cored, and sliced

1 large onion, thinly sliced

3 large potatoes, peeled and
thinly sliced

1 teaspoon packed brown sugar

1 teaspoon grated orange zest

Sea salt and freshly ground black
pepper

1 cup chicken broth

Preheat the oven to 350°F. Grease an ovenproof casserole dish large enough to hold the chops in a single layer.

Sprinkle the chops with the chile seasoning. In a large skillet, combine the oil and 1 tablespoon of the butter. Place over medium heat until the butter melts. Add the pork and sauté for 5 minutes, or until lightly browned on both sides. Transfer to a plate.

In the same skillet, sauté the apples and onion for about 5 minutes, or until lightly colored.

Layer half of the potatoes in the prepared casserole. Top with the chops and spoon the apple mixture over them. Sprinkle with the brown sugar, orange zest, salt, and pepper. Cover with the rest of the potatoes and pour the stock over them. Dot with the remaining 1 tablespoon butter.

Bake for 45 minutes, until the potatoes are tender and golden brown.

Lavender Breast of Chicken
Stuffed with Apples and Fennel in Parchment

Foods cooked en papillote—*meaning in parchment paper—have a high wow factor. They impress guests first with their appearance and then with the heavenly aromas that are released when the paper packets are opened. Here, lavender really accents the apple and fennel.*

The best way to open the baked packets: With the tines of a fork, make a small slit to allow the steam to escape. Then make the hole bigger and tear open the packet. Enjoy!

MAKES 6 SERVINGS

4 tablespoons unsalted butter

3 tablespoons extra-virgin olive oil

3 apples, peeled, cored, and finely diced

1 leek, cut in half lengthwise and thinly sliced (white and pale green parts only)

1 small fennel bulb, diced

2 tablespoons chopped garlic

¼ cup fresh Italian parsley leaves, coarsely chopped

1 tablespoon grated lemon zest

6 bone-in chicken breast halves with skin

Sea salt and freshly ground black pepper

½ cup dry white wine

¼ cup lavender honey or honey

6 lemon slices

2 tablespoons dried culinary 'Provence' lavender buds, finely ground in a spice grinder

Preheat the oven to 350°F.

Melt the butter in a large skillet over medium heat. Add the oil, apples, leek, and fennel. Sauté for 3 minutes, or until just tender. Add the garlic and sauté for 3 minutes. Mix in the parsley and lemon zest.

Cut six 12 x 8-inch sheets of parchment paper. Lay the sheets on a work surface with the long sides facing you. Butter the paper. Place ¼ cup of the leek mixture slightly off-center on each piece of paper. Top with the chicken, skin side up, and sprinkle with salt and pepper. Peel back the skin and place 1 tablespoon of the leek mixture over the meat; replace the skin.

In a cup, mix the wine and honey. Spoon over the chicken. Top each breast with a lemon slice and sprinkle with the lavender.

Fold the parchment over the chicken, letting the three edges meet. Fold all three edges inward toward the chicken until you form a tight package. Place the packages on a baking sheet and bake for 35 minutes.

To serve, place each packet on a dinner plate. Let diners open their own packages at the table.

CHILI LAVENDER TURKEY POT PIE
WITH SPICY CRUST

Pot pies are old-fashioned comfort food. This updated version adds lots of vegetables and Southwestern spices. The real surprise is the lavender and spices in the crust.

You can easily prepare the filling a day ahead and top it with the crust just before baking. Increase the baking time to 1 hour.

MAKES 8 SERVINGS

Spicy Pot Pie Crust (recipe follows)
1 (1-pound) acorn squash, peeled
    and cubed (see note)
1 medium carrot, diced
¼ cup vegetable oil
1 large onion, diced
2 tablespoons minced garlic
1 tablespoon chipotle chile powder
1 tablespoon Spiced Lavender
    Seasoning (page 18)
1 red bell pepper, cubed
1 green bell pepper, cubed
1 cup frozen white corn kernels
2 (28-ounce) cans chopped
    tomatoes, undrained
1¼ pounds cooked turkey breast,
    cubed
1 (19-ounce) can black beans,
    rinsed and drained
⅓ cup fresh cilantro leaves,
    chopped
Sea salt and freshly ground black
    pepper

Prepare the pie crust.

Bring a large pot of salted water to a boil. Add the squash and cook for 6 minutes, or until tender. Using a slotted spoon, transfer to a colander. Add the carrot to the pot and cook for 4 minutes, or until tender. Pour into the colander.

Warm the oil in a large skillet over medium heat. Add the onion, garlic, chile powder, and lavender seasoning. Sauté for 5 minutes, or until the onion is translucent.

Add the red pepper, green pepper, and corn. Sauté for 5 minutes. Add the tomatoes and bring to a simmer. Simmer for 10 minutes, stirring occasionally. Stir in the squash, carrot, turkey, beans, and cilantro. Cook for 3 minutes, or until heated through. Season with salt and pepper.

Transfer the mixture to a deep 3½- to 4-quart baking dish. Let cool for 30 minutes.

Preheat the oven to 350°F.

On a lightly floured surface, roll out the dough to the size of the dish. Place the crust on top of the filling, sealing the edges to the rim of the dish. Cut one or two steam holes in the crust.

Bake for 30 to 40 minutes, or until the crust is golden brown and the filling is bubbly. Let cool for 5 minutes before serving.

 Acorn squash can be tricky to peel because of the ridges. Just use a sharp vegetable peeler and take your time.

Spicy Pot Pie Crust

2½ cups all-purpose flour

2 teaspoons chili powder

2 teaspoons ground cumin

2 teaspoons dried culinary
   'Provence' lavender buds, finely
   ground in a spice grinder

2 teaspoons onion powder

2 teaspoons paprika

1 teaspoon sea salt

½ pound (2 sticks) cold unsalted
   butter, cut into cubes

¼ cup ice water

In the bowl of a food processor, combine the flour, chili powder, cumin, lavender, onion powder, paprika, and salt. Pulse to combine. Sprinkle the butter over the surface. Pulse just until the mixture resembles coarse crumbs. Add the water and pulse just until the dough starts to clump together. Gather the dough into a ball and form into a flattened disk. Wrap in plastic wrap and refrigerate until needed.

VEAL SCALOPPINE AND ARTICHOKE HEARTS
WITH POMEGRANATE LAVENDER SAUCE

The unusual flavor combination of lavender and pomegranate delightfully enhances an old favorite. Try this imaginative combination on a chilly fall evening. Serve with Hot Spiced Lavender Red Cabbage Slaw (page 135) and Risotto-Style Yukon Gold Potatoes with Lavender and Rosemary (page 175).

MAKES 4 TO 6 SERVINGS

3 tablespoons fresh thyme leaves

2 tablespoons black peppercorns,
  coarsely ground

1 teaspoon dried culinary
  'Provence' lavender buds, finely
  ground in a spice grinder

6 garlic cloves, minced

9 tablespoons extra-virgin olive oil

1½ pounds veal scaloppine, no
  more than ⅛ inch thick

Pomegranate Lavender Sauce
  (recipe follows)

1 cup all-purpose flour

4 tablespoons unsalted butter

1 cup frozen artichoke hearts,
  thawed and cut into quarters

1 lemon, thinly sliced (garnish)

Fresh thyme sprigs (garnish)

Fresh lavender sprigs (garnish)

In a small bowl, mix the thyme, peppercorns, lavender, garlic, and 2 tablespoons of the oil. Rub the veal all over with the mixture. Cover and refrigerate for 3 hours.

Prepare the pomegranate sauce.

Place the flour on a plate and dip the veal in it to coat both sides; shake off the excess. Place the butter and 5 tablespoons oil in a large skillet over high heat. Working in batches, add a single layer of veal and sauté for 1 minute, or until slightly browned; turn and sauté for 1 minute or less on the other side, until cooked through. Transfer to the middle of a serving platter, slightly overlapping the slices. Cover with foil to keep warm.

In the same skillet, warm the remaining 2 tablespoons oil over medium-low heat. Add the artichoke hearts and cook for 5 minutes, or until tender and starting to brown. Using tongs, arrange the artichokes around the veal.

Pour some of the sauce over the veal and artichokes. Garnish with the lemon slices, thyme sprigs, and lavender sprigs. Serve the remaining sauce at the table.

POMEGRANATE LAVENDER SAUCE

3 slices pancetta, finely chopped

I tablespoon extra-virgin olive oil

4 shallots, minced

½ cup dry red wine

3 tablespoons orange juice

I cup chicken broth

2 tablespoons tomato paste

I tablespoon pomegranate molasses
 (see note)

I teaspoon dried culinary
 'Provence' lavender buds, finely
 ground in a spice grinder

¼ cup heavy cream (optional)

Sea salt and freshly ground black
 pepper

In a medium saucepan over medium-high heat, sauté the pancetta in the oil for 3 minutes, or until crisp. Add the shallots and sauté for 1 minute. Add the wine and orange juice. Cook until only 2 tablespoons of liquid remain. Stir in the broth, tomato paste, molasses, lavender, and cream (if using). Bring to a boil and cook for 7 minutes, or until the sauce is reduced to 1 cup. Season with salt and pepper.

Pomegranate molasses is available at most international and Middle Eastern food markets. You can also order it at www.deandeluca.com.

HOT SPICED LAVENDER RED CABBAGE SLAW

Sweet, sour, spicy, crunchy! Add this coleslaw to a regular weeknight menu and watch their eyes light up.

MAKES 8 SERVINGS

½ pound thick-sliced bacon, diced
1 cup finely diced yellow onion
1 tablespoon dried culinary
    'Provence' lavender buds, finely
    ground in a spice grinder
1 teaspoon caraway seeds
1 teaspoon mustard seeds
1 tablespoon all-purpose flour
⅔ cup white wine vinegar
⅓ cup sugar
¼ cup chicken broth
Sea salt and freshly ground black
    pepper
8 cups thinly shredded red cabbage
2 green apples, peeled, cored,
    and shredded
¼ cup fresh Italian parsley leaves,
    chopped

Fry the bacon in a large skillet over medium heat until crisp. Pour off all but ¼ cup of the drippings. Add the onion, lavender, caraway seeds, and mustard seeds to the skillet. Cook for 5 minutes, or until the onion softens. Whisk in the flour and cook for 1 to 2 minutes to remove the starchy taste of the flour.

Stir in the vinegar, sugar, and broth. Season with salt and pepper. Add the cabbage and apples. Cook for 4 to 5 minutes, tossing the cabbage with tongs to wilt it. Stir in the parsley just before serving.

Jasmine Rice Mushroom Pilaf
with Lavender

Add the subtle scent of lavender to aromatic jasmine rice and you get a new side dish that's fit for company—and easy enough for quick weeknight meals. Take your choice of mushrooms. Cremini and shiitake are especially good.

I like to prepare this pilaf in a rice cooker. If you don't have one, use a covered 2-quart casserole dish and bake the rice at 350°F for 20 to 25 minutes.

MAKES 6 SERVINGS

1 tablespoon dried culinary 'Provence' lavender buds
2 teaspoons mustard seeds
$\frac{1}{2}$ teaspoon fennel seeds
2 tablespoons extra-virgin olive oil
$\frac{1}{4}$ pound mixed mushrooms, diced
1 cup uncooked jasmine rice
$\frac{1}{2}$ cup finely diced shallot
$\frac{1}{2}$ cup finely diced green onion
$\frac{1}{2}$ teaspoon sea salt
$\frac{1}{4}$ teaspoon freshly ground black pepper
2 cups reduced-sodium chicken broth

Combine the lavender, mustard seeds, and fennel seeds in a spice grinder. Pulse until finely ground.

Warm the oil in a large skillet over medium-high heat. Add the mushrooms and sauté for 7 minutes, or until golden and the liquid released by the mushrooms evaporates. Add the rice, shallot, green onion, salt, pepper, and lavender mixture.

Transfer to a rice cooker and add the chicken broth. Cook for 30 minutes, or until the rice is tender and the liquid has been absorbed.

Raspberry Blueberry Bread Pudding

An abundance of berries makes this bread pudding light and refreshing. The aromatic quality of lavender plays lightly off the berry flavors. And the rich, sweet sauce sets off the tartness of the fruit.

Both the bread pudding and the sauce can be made ahead. The bread pudding even freezes very well. To reheat the bread pudding, let it thaw in the refrigerator and then bake it uncovered at 350°F for 20 to 30 minutes, until heated through. Rewarm the sauce by whisking it in a double boiler or carefully heating in the microwave.

MAKES 6 SERVINGS

I tablespoon dried culinary
   'Provence' lavender buds
2 cups sugar
2 teaspoons ground cinnamon
$\frac{1}{4}$ teaspoon salt
I quart milk
I tablespoon vanilla extract
$1\frac{1}{2}$ pounds brioche or challah,
   torn into small pieces
4 large eggs, slightly beaten
$\frac{1}{4}$ pound (I stick) unsalted butter,
   melted
2 (10-ounce) packages frozen
   unsweetened raspberries, thawed
I pint fresh blueberries
Vanilla Lavender Sauce
   (recipe follows)

Preheat the oven to 375°F. Butter a 13 x 9-inch baking dish.

Combine the lavender and $\frac{1}{4}$ cup of the sugar in a spice grinder. Pulse until finely ground. Transfer to a small bowl and stir in the cinnamon, salt, and the remaining $1\frac{3}{4}$ cups sugar.

In a large bowl, mix the milk and vanilla. Add the bread, mix well, and let soak for 15 minutes, stirring occasionally. Stir in the eggs and then the butter. Stir in the sugar mixture. Gently stir in the raspberries (with juices) and blueberries. Pour into the prepared baking dish.

Bake for I hour, or until the center is just slightly wiggly and the top is lightly browned.

Prepare the vanilla sauce. Serve warm with the warm bread pudding.

Vanilla Lavender Sauce

I teaspoon dried culinary
   'Provence' lavender buds
I cup sugar
$\frac{1}{4}$ pound (I stick) unsalted butter
$\frac{1}{2}$ cup half-and-half
$1\frac{1}{2}$ teaspoons vanilla extract
I tablespoon orange liqueur
   (optional)

Combine the lavender and $\frac{1}{4}$ cup of the sugar in a spice grinder. Pulse until finely ground. Transfer to the top of a double boiler or a metal bowl that fits atop a saucepan. Add the butter, half-and-half, vanilla, liqueur (if using), and the remaining $\frac{3}{4}$ cup sugar. Whisk over simmering water for 5 minutes, or until the butter melts and the sauce thickens slightly. Serve warm.

Lavender Fruit Mosaic Tart

This sumptuous tart encompasses a virtual cornucopia of seasonal fruits and nuts, making it perfect for Thanksgiving and the later holidays. Lavishly spiced with a hint of lavender and notes of brandy or rum, this substantial dessert is a paean to the opulence of autumn.

MAKES 16 SERVINGS

Lavender Pecan Crust
   (recipe follows)
1 medium pear (preferably Anjou
   or Bosc), peeled, cored, and
   finely diced
1 medium apple, peeled, cored,
   and finely diced
1 cup dried currants
1 cup seedless green grapes,
   cut in half
½ cup sweetened dried cranberries
½ cup toasted pecans, coarsely
   chopped
¼ cup dried apricots, finely diced
¼ cup golden raisins
3 tablespoons chopped candied
   orange zest
2 tablespoons dried culinary
   'Provence' lavender buds, finely
   ground in a spice grinder
Zest and juice of 1 lemon
¼ teaspoon ground cinnamon
⅛ teaspoon grated nutmeg
½ cup packed dark brown sugar
¼ cup lavender honey or honey
¼ cup brandy or rum
2 tablespoons unsalted butter,
   melted
2 large eggs
2 tablespoons milk
1 tablespoon all-purpose flour
Lavender Whipped Cream
   (recipe follows)

Prepare the dough for the crust.

In a large saucepan, mix the pear, apple, currants, grapes, cranberries, pecans, apricots, raisins, orange zest, lavender, lemon zest, lemon juice, cinnamon, and nutmeg. Stir in the brown sugar, honey, brandy or rum, and butter. Cook over medium heat for 7 minutes, or until the fruit is tender. Cool.

Preheat the oven to 375°F.

Press the dough into a 9-inch tart pan with a removable bottom. Trim the edges. Add the cooled fruit filling.

In a small bowl, mix the eggs, milk, and flour. Pour over the filling (be careful not to overfill the tart shell).

Bake for 30 to 40 minutes, or until the filling is set and golden brown.

While the tart bakes, prepare the whipped cream. Serve the tart warm or at room temperature with the whipped cream.

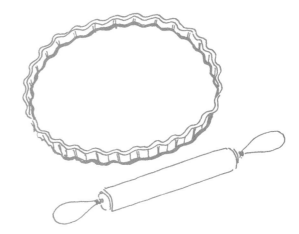

Lavender Pecan Crust

1½ cups all-purpose flour

1 cup pecans

3 tablespoons sugar

1 tablespoon dried culinary 'Provence' lavender buds, finely ground in a spice grinder

⅛ teaspoon salt

¼ pound (1 stick) cold unsalted butter, cut into small pieces

1 large egg yolk

1 tablespoon ice water

In the bowl of a food processor, combine the flour, pecans, sugar, lavender, and salt. Pulse until the nuts are finely ground. Scatter the butter over the flour and pulse until the mixture resembles coarse crumbs.

In a cup, beat the egg yolk and water with a fork to combine. Add to the food processor and pulse until a dough forms. Gather the dough into a ball and form into a flattened disk with your hands. Wrap in plastic wrap and refrigerate for at least 30 minutes.

For variety, replace the pecans in the crust and filling with unsalted pistachio nuts.

Lavender Whipped Cream

½ cup heavy cream

1 tablespoon Lavender Sugar (page 19)

1 tablespoon brandy or rum

Place the cream in a chilled medium bowl. Add the lavender sugar and brandy or rum. Beat with chilled beaters until thick.

Lavender Honey Custard Ice Cream

Flower-scented ice cream must have been a dream of the gods. Distinctive notes of lavender take this rich and velvety concoction to a new realm. Although lovely on its own, it's the perfect accompaniment to hot apple pie, bread pudding, or Lavender Fruit Mosaic Tart (page 138). This recipe is an adaptation of one given to me by my student and good friend Richard Sweet.

MAKES ABOUT 4 CUPS

¾ cup milk
⅓ cup honey
1 tablespoon dried culinary 'Provence' lavender buds
1½ cups heavy cream
½ vanilla bean, cut in half lengthwise
10 large egg yolks
⅔ cup sugar
1 tablespoon vanilla extract

In a medium saucepan, whisk together the milk, honey, lavender, and ¾ cup of the cream. Add the vanilla bean. Heat, stirring often, until small bubbles start to form around the edge; do not boil. Set aside to cool slightly.

In a large bowl, combine the egg yolks and sugar. Beat with an electric mixer for 5 minutes, or the mixture is a light lemony yellow and forms a slowly dissolving ribbon when the beater is lifted.

Slowly beat in the milk mixture. Pour back into the saucepan. Use a paring knife to scrape the seeds from the vanilla bean and add them to the pan. Cook over medium heat, stirring constantly, until the mixture thickens and reaches 175°F on an instant-read thermometer (don't go above 180°F or the eggs will curdle).

Strain into a medium bowl. Place over a larger bowl containing ice cubes and cold water. Stir often until cool. Stir in the vanilla extract and the remaining ¾ cup cream. Transfer to an ice cream maker and freeze according to the manufacturer's directions.

Oatmeal Cookie Bars
with Lavender Fig Cheesecake Filling

Heavenly doesn't begin to describe these unusual cookie bars. A buttery pecan and oat crust joins forces with a creamy fig filling. The hint of lavender makes them totally irresistible.

MAKES 15 BARS

Oat Pecan Crust (recipe follows)
3 (8-ounce) packages cream cheese,
    at room temperature
1/4 cup sugar
3 large eggs
6 tablespoons half-and-half
    or milk
2 tablespoons fresh lemon juice
1 1/2 teaspoons dried culinary
    'Provence' lavender buds, finely
    ground in a spice grinder
1 tablespoon vanilla extract
1/4 cup fig puree (see note)

Preheat the oven to 350°F. Grease a 13 x 9-inch baking dish.

Prepare the crust mixture. Press evenly into the bottom of the prepared baking dish.

Bake for 18 to 20 minutes, or until light brown.

Combine the cream cheese and sugar in a large bowl. Beat with an electric mixer until smooth. Beat in the eggs, half-and-half or milk, lemon juice, lavender, and vanilla.

Transfer 2 cups of the filling to a small bowl and stir in the fig puree.

Pour the remaining filling over the baked crust. Drop spoonfuls of the fig mixture into the baking dish. Run a knife through the filling to lightly swirl the mixtures.

Bake for 25 minutes. Cool to room temperature. Refrigerate until cold and cut into squares.

Fig puree is available from Orchard Choice (Valley Fig Growers) in Fresno, California. To order, call (559) 237-3893.

Oat Pecan Crust

3/4 cup chopped toasted pecans
3/4 cup packed light brown sugar
3/4 cup quick-cooking rolled oats
1/2 teaspoon ground cinnamon
4 tablespoons unsalted butter,
    melted

In a food processor, grind the pecans and brown sugar until an even texture. Transfer to a medium bowl and stir in the oats and cinnamon. Stir in the butter.

WINTER LAVENDER

Warming and Hearty

CONTENTS

LAVENDER CHICKEN ROLLS
WITH GREEN ONIONS AND RED PEPPERS

These appetizers abound with Pacific Rim flavors. Tender chicken takes on a taste of Asia and produces succulent bite-size morsels.

Be sure to use Asian (dark) sesame seed oil, which is very flavorful. Look for it—as well as mirin, plum sauce, chile-garlic sauce, and black sesame seeds—at Japanese markets, natural food stores, and supermarkets with a well-stocked Asian foods section.

MAKES ABOUT 30 ROLLS

Marinade
½ cup mirin (rice wine)
¼ cup soy sauce
¼ cup plum sauce
2 tablespoons superfine sugar
2 tablespoons rice vinegar
2 tablespoons Asian sesame oil
1 tablespoon grated fresh ginger
1 tablespoon Asian chile-garlic sauce
1 teaspoon dried culinary 'Provence' lavender buds, finely ground in a spice grinder

Chicken Rolls
4 large boneless, skinless chicken breast halves
2 green onions, cut in half lengthwise
1 (6½-ounce) jar roasted red bell peppers, drained and cut into ⅓-inch slices
Spicy Lavender Dipping Sauce (recipe follows)
½ cup black sesame seeds, toasted
1 cup white sesame seeds, toasted

To make the marinade: In a small bowl, whisk together the mirin, soy sauce, plum sauce, sugar, vinegar, sesame oil, ginger, chile sauce, and lavender until the sugar dissolves.

To make the chicken: Place each breast between two pieces of parchment paper. Use the smooth side of a meat pounder to flatten the breasts until they are slightly less than ¼ inch thick. Arrange skin side down on a work surface.

For each roll, place a green onion half lengthwise down the center of the breast; trim the excess onion. Put 2 pepper slices on top of the onion. Fold in the ends of the breast to even them, then roll lengthwise to form a long cylinder. Place seam side down in a baking dish large enough to hold the rolls in a single layer.

Pour the marinade over the chicken, turn the rolls carefully to coat, and let marinate for 45 minutes.

Wrap each roll securely in plastic wrap. (The wrapped rolls may be made up to 1 day ahead and kept in the refrigerator.)

Place a bamboo steamer over a wok half-filled with boiling water. Unwrap the rolls and set in the steamer. Cover and cook for 5 minutes, or until firm to the touch. Remove from the steamer and let cool. Refrigerate for at least 2 hours or overnight.

Prepare the dipping sauce.

Roll the cylinders in the sesame seeds to coat. Trim the ends diagonally and cut into 1-inch pieces. Turn the pieces cut side up and arrange decoratively on a platter. Serve with the dipping sauce.

For an impressive presentation, stick a bamboo skewer into each appetizer and arrange on a platter.

Spicy Lavender Dipping Sauce

³/₄ cup rice vinegar

¹/₂ cup sugar

¹/₂ teaspoon cornstarch

¹/₄ teaspoon sea salt

1 red bell pepper, finely diced

¹/₂ teaspoon crushed hot-pepper
flakes

1¹/₂ teaspoons dried culinary
'Provence' lavender buds, finely
ground in a spice grinder

1 tablespoon finely chopped fresh
cilantro leaves

In a medium saucepan, whisk together the vinegar, sugar, cornstarch, and salt to dissolve the sugar and cornstarch. Add the bell pepper, pepper flakes, and lavender. Whisk over medium heat for 5 minutes, or until the sauce thickens. Let cool to room temperature and stir in the cilantro. (Or refrigerate for up to 1 day, bring to room temperature, and stir in the cilantro.)

Lavender Coconut Pork Bites
with Spicy Peanut Sauce

An Asian influence is evident in these little cubes. Coconut and brown sugar balance the spices with sweetness. Lavender adds an unexpected interesting note.

MAKES 50 SERVINGS

2 pounds pork tenderloin
1 cup unsweetened coconut milk
2 tablespoons fresh lime juice
1 tablespoon Asian chile-garlic
   sauce
1 tablespoon dried mint
2 teaspoons ground cumin
1½ teaspoons dried culinary
   'Provence' lavender buds, finely
   ground in a spice grinder
¾ teaspoon ground coriander
½ teaspoon cayenne pepper
1 garlic clove, crushed
Sea salt and freshly ground black
   pepper
1 cup sweetened shredded coconut
2 cups roasted peanuts
Spicy Lavender Coconut Peanut
   Sauce (recipe follows)

Trim any fat from the pork and cut the meat into long, 1-inch-wide strips. In a large bowl, mix the coconut milk, lime juice, chile sauce, mint, cumin, lavender, coriander, cayenne, and garlic. Season with salt and pepper. Add the pork and mix well. Cover and refrigerate for at least 2 hours or overnight.

Preheat the oven to 375°F.

Spread the coconut on a rimmed baking sheet. Bake, stirring occasionally, for 15 minutes, or until golden brown. Let cool and place in a shallow bowl. In a food processor, chop the peanuts medium coarsely and mix with the coconut.

Prepare the peanut sauce. If not using immediately, cover and refrigerate. Reheat before using.

Preheat a grill to hot.

Transfer the pork to the grill rack (discard any remaining marinade). Grill for 6 to 7 minutes per side, or until cooked through. Cut into 1-inch cubes.

Place half of the peanut sauce in a shallow bowl. Dip the cubes into the peanut sauce and then roll in the coconut and peanut mixture. Use two-pronged Asian picks, available at Asian markets, to serve the cubes. Serve with the remaining peanut sauce for dipping.

SPICY LAVENDER COCONUT PEANUT SAUCE

2 tablespoons peanut oil

1 small white onion, finely diced

2 teaspoons grated fresh ginger

1 garlic clove, minced

1 cup unsweetened coconut milk

1/4 cup smooth peanut butter

Juice of 1 lemon

1 tablespoon light or regular soy
    sauce

2 teaspoons dried culinary
    'Provence' lavender buds, finely
    ground in a spice grinder

1 jalapeño pepper, seeded and
    finely diced

Pinch of dark brown sugar

Sea salt and freshly ground black
    pepper

Warm the peanut oil in a small saucepan over medium heat. Add the onion, ginger, and garlic. Sauté for 5 minutes, or until soft and golden. Whisk in the coconut milk, peanut butter, lemon juice, soy sauce, lavender, jalapeño, and brown sugar. Season with salt and pepper. Stirring continuously, simmer for 3 to 4 minutes.

GARLICKY LAVENDER CURRY HUMMUS
WITH PITA CRISPS

Why buy supermarket hummus and pita chips when you can easily make much better ones at home? If you prepare the chips ahead, store them at room temperature in an airtight container. The hummus is also good with raw vegetables and even with warmed soft pita bread.

MAKES 24 SERVINGS

Lavender Pita Crisps
   (recipe follows)
2 (15-ounce) cans garbanzo beans,
   rinsed and drained
²⁄₃ cup tahini (sesame paste) or
   creamy peanut butter
¹⁄₃ cup water
¹⁄₃ cup fresh lemon juice
2 tablespoons extra-virgin olive oil
2 teaspoons dried culinary
   'Provence' lavender buds, finely
   ground in a spice grinder
1¹⁄₂ teaspoons Madras or regular
   curry powder (see note)
¹⁄₂ teaspoon sea salt
2 large garlic cloves, minced
Paprika
Chopped fresh Italian parsley leaves

Prepare the pita crisps.

In a food processor, combine the beans, tahini or peanut butter, water, lemon juice, oil, lavender, curry powder, salt, and garlic. Process until smooth, adding more water as needed to reach a dip consistency. Season with additional salt and lemon juice, if needed. Transfer to a shallow serving bowl and dust with the paprika and parsley. Serve with the pita crisps.

Madras curry powder is hotter than the standard spice-aisle blend.

LAVENDER PITA CRISPS

¾ cup extra-virgin olive oil

2 tablespoons dried parsley

1 tablespoon fresh lemon juice

2 teaspoons Spiced Lavender
 Seasoning (page 18)

1 medium garlic clove, minced

6 pita breads (6 to 7 inches in
 diameter)

In a small bowl, mix the oil, parsley, lemon juice, chile seasoning, and garlic. Cover and let stand at room temperature for at least 1 hour.

Preheat the oven to 400°F.

Cut each pita bread in half and then into thirds, making 6 triangles. Separate the two layers of each triangle. Brush the rough side of each triangle with the oil mixture. Arrange, oil side up, in a single layer on baking sheets.

Bake for 9 to 10 minutes, or until just crisp and lightly browned at the edges. Let cool.

For variety, brush the pita triangles with olive oil and season lightly with dried herbs (such as dill), spices (such as cumin), or even Parmesan cheese.

Northwest Lavender Crab Cakes
with Creamy Honey Sauce

Fresh crabmeat tastes naturally sweet with a hint of ocean saltiness. These flavors are enhanced by a fragrant honey and lavender sauce.

For a smashing presentation, place the sauce in a pastry bag fitted with a star tip and pipe the sauce onto the finished crab cakes. To turn these appetizers into a main course, just form the mixture into four larger patties.

MAKES 8 SERVINGS

¼ cup minced celery
¼ cup minced green onion
¼ cup mayonnaise
1 large egg
1 tablespoon dry mustard
2 teaspoons dried culinary
    'Provence' lavender buds, finely
    ground in a spice grinder
¼ teaspoon sea salt
Generous pinch of cayenne pepper
1 pound fresh crabmeat
2¾ cups panko (see note)
Creamy Honey Lavender Sauce
    (recipe follows)
2 tablespoons unsalted butter
2 tablespoons extra-virgin olive oil
Lemon wedges (garnish)
Chopped fresh Italian parsley
    leaves (garnish)

In a medium bowl, mix the celery, green onion, mayonnaise, egg, mustard, lavender, salt, and cayenne. Pick through the crabmeat to remove any pieces of shell or cartilage. Stir the crab into the bowl. Mix in enough panko (about 1 cup) to form a mixture that barely holds together. Place the remaining panko in a shallow bowl.

Shape the crab mixture into 8 patties about ¾ inch thick. Press into the panko to coat on all sides. Place on a plate, cover with plastic wrap, and refrigerate for at least 1 hour.

Prepare the honey sauce, cover, and refrigerate until needed.

Combine 1 tablespoon of the butter and 1 tablespoon of the oil in a large skillet and place over medium-high heat until the butter melts. Add 4 crab cakes, reduce the heat to medium, and cook for 4 minutes per side, or until browned. Wipe the skillet clean with paper towels. Repeat to use the remaining butter, oil, and crab cakes. Transfer to appetizer plates and garnish with lemon wedges. Add dollops of the sauce and sprinkle with parsley.

Panko are Japanese bread crumbs that are light in color and weight. Because they're coarse textured, they make a crispy crust.

CREAMY HONEY LAVENDER SAUCE

1 cup mayonnaise
¼ cup sour cream
¼ cup lavender honey or honey
2 tablespoons fresh cilantro leaves,
    chopped
1 tablespoon fresh lemon juice
1 tablespoon Dijon mustard
1 teaspoon dried culinary
    'Provence' lavender buds, finely
    ground in a spice grinder
Sea salt and freshly ground black
    pepper

In a small bowl, whisk together the mayonnaise, sour cream, honey, cilantro, lemon juice, mustard, and lavender. Season with salt and pepper.

OLIVE LAVENDER COUNTRY BREAD

This bread represents the very soul of Provence. Nothing speaks of a French table like a warm, herb-scented loaf of bread, straight from the oven. Served with a favorite soup, this is perfect for chilly fall and winter days.

MAKES 2 LOAVES

1 cup warm water (about 110° to 115°F)

2½ teaspoons (1 package) active dried yeast

1 cup milk, heated to 180°F and cooled to lukewarm

⅔ cup coarsely chopped onion

⅔ cup Niçoise olives, pitted and coarsely chopped

3 tablespoons unsalted butter, at room temperature

2 tablespoons dried culinary 'Provence' lavender buds, finely ground in a spice grinder

2 tablespoons sugar

1 tablespoon freshly ground black pepper

2 teaspoons sea salt

½ cup plus 2 tablespoons yellow cornmeal

2 cups whole wheat flour

3 to 3½ cups unbleached bread flour

Place the water in a large bowl and sprinkle with the yeast. Set aside for 5 minutes, or until foamy. Stir in the milk and then the onion, olives, butter, lavender, sugar, pepper, salt, and ½ cup of the cornmeal. Add the whole wheat flour and beat well.

Add enough of the bread flour to make a dough that pulls away from the sides of the bowl. Turn out onto a lightly floured surface and knead for 2 to 3 minutes, adding more bread flour to make a workable dough. Drape with a piece of plastic wrap and let rest for 10 to 15 minutes.

Knead the dough for about 10 minutes, or until smooth and elastic; sprinkle it with flour as you knead to keep it from sticking.

Lightly oil a large bowl. Place the dough in the bowl and turn to coat all sides. Cover the bowl with plastic wrap and let the dough rise in a warm draft-free place for 1½ hours, or until doubled in size.

Punch down the dough and divide in half. Knead each half briefly and then shape into a round loaf. Dust a pizza peel with the remaining 2 tablespoons cornmeal. Place the loaves on the peel, smooth side up. Cover with a lightly floured kitchen towel and let rise for 45 minutes, or until barely doubled in size.

Place a pizza stone on the center oven rack and preheat the oven to 350°F.

Slide the loaves onto the stone and bake for 45 minutes, or until the loaves are well browned and sound hollow when the bottom is tapped with your finger. Let cool on a wire rack.

Lavender Blueberry Banana Bread

On a cold winter's day, fill your kitchen with the scent of baking bananas and blueberries. It's real comfort food. Toast a few slices of the bread and serve with Lavender Butter (page 21).

MAKES 1 LOAF

¼ pound (1 stick) unsalted butter,
    at room temperature
⅔ cup sugar
2 large eggs
1 cup all-purpose flour
1 tablespoon dried culinary
    'Provence' lavender buds, finely
    ground in a spice grinder
1 teaspoon baking soda
½ teaspoon salt
1 cup whole wheat flour
3 large ripe bananas, mashed
1¼ cups blueberries
½ cup walnuts, coarsely chopped
1 teaspoon vanilla extract

Preheat the oven to 350°F. Grease a 9 x 5-inch loaf pan or coat with nonstick spray.

In a large bowl, combine the butter and sugar. Beat with an electric mixer until fluffy. Add the eggs one at a time, beating well after each addition.

Sift the all-purpose flour, lavender, baking soda, and salt into a medium bowl. Stir in the whole wheat flour. Beat into the butter mixture. Fold in the bananas, blueberries, walnuts, and vanilla. Pour into the prepared pan.

Bake for 50 to 60 minutes, or until a cake tester inserted in the center comes out clean. Cool in the pan for 10 minutes. Remove from the pan and cool on a wire rack.

Lemon Lavender Bourbon Toddy

This will warm you up when you need it most! And the sunny tart flavor of lemon will lift you out of the winter doldrums.

MAKES 8 TO 12 SERVINGS

6 cups water
3 cups sugar
1 tablespoon dried culinary
    'Provence' lavender buds
4½ cups fresh lemon juice
2¼ cups bourbon
Cinnamon sticks (garnish)
Lemon slices (garnish)

In a large saucepan, mix the water, sugar, and lavender. Bring to a boil over high heat and stir to dissolve the sugar. Cover, remove from the heat, and let steep for 5 minutes.

Strain out the lavender and return the liquid to the saucepan. Add the lemon juice and bourbon. Bring just to a simmer over medium heat. Serve in mugs and garnish with cinnamon sticks or lemon slices.

Lavender Hot Cocoa

I was surprised how lavender enriches the flavor of chocolate. Even before you take a sip, your nose catches a whiff of something different. Then the soft note of lavender plays across your tongue, and the full chocolate orchestra fills your mouth. Creamy, rich, and satisfying, this is the kind of drink you appreciate at the end of a long cold day.

MAKES 4 SERVINGS

¼ cup unsweetened Dutch-process
    cocoa powder (see note)
3 tablespoons sugar
⅛ teaspoon salt
1 quart milk
1 teaspoon dried culinary
    'Provence' lavender buds, finely
    ground in a spice grinder
1 ounce bittersweet or semisweet
    chocolate, finely chopped
1 teaspoon vanilla extract

In a small bowl, mix the cocoa, sugar, and salt.

In a medium saucepan, combine the milk and lavender. Bring just to a simmer. Remove from the heat and let steep for about 10 minutes. Strain and return to the saucepan. Bring to a simmer again and remove from the heat. Whisk in the chocolate until it's melted. Whisk in the vanilla and the cocoa mixture. Serve immediately.

Dutch-process cocoa has been treated with an alkali to neutralize cocoa's natural acidity. It tends to be darker and richer than regular cocoa. Look for it in the baking aisle with other cocoa powder.

MEATBALL, LEEK, AND SPINACH SOUP

This is a soup that will warm you up in no time! It's a traditional Italian wedding soup—with a twist: lavender. It's substantial because of the meatballs. The leeks and spinach are full of important vitamins. And the lavender adds irresistible flavor.

MAKES 8 SERVINGS

**Lavender Mini-Meatballs
    (recipe follows)**
6 tablespoons unsalted butter
¼ cup extra-virgin olive oil
**2 leeks, cut in half lengthwise
    and diced (white and pale
    green parts only)**
1 fennel bulb, diced
8 cups chicken broth
**1 tablespoon Glace de Poulet Gold
    (see note)**
1 cup dry pastina pasta
**Sea salt and freshly ground black
    pepper**
⅔ cup packed spinach leaves
Grated Parmesan cheese

Prepare the meatballs.

Melt the butter in a large pot over medium heat. Add the oil, leeks, and fennel. Sauté for 15 minutes, or until just translucent. Add the broth and glace de poulet. Cover and simmer for 20 minutes, or until the vegetables are tender.

Drop in the meatballs. When the meatballs rise to the surface, add the pastina and simmer until tender. Season with salt and pepper. Add the spinach just before serving and stir until limp. Serve with cheese sprinkled on top.

Glace de Poulet Gold is a chicken-stock concentrate. It enriches the flavor of regular broth or stock. You can find this product at most upscale supermarkets and specialty food stores or at www.morethangourmet.com.

LAVENDER MINI-MEATBALLS

½ pound ground beef or veal
½ cup chopped onion
1 large egg
**2 tablespoons grated Parmesan
    cheese**
2 tablespoons dried bread crumbs
**1 teaspoon dried culinary
    'Provence' lavender buds, finely
    ground in a spice grinder**
½ teaspoon sea salt
**⅛ teaspoon freshly ground black
    pepper**

In a medium bowl, mix the beef or veal, onion, egg, cheese, bread crumbs, lavender, salt, and pepper. Form into ½-inch meatballs and set aside.

CREAM OF CHESTNUT SOUP
WITH LAVENDER GARNISH

Creamy, aromatic chestnut soup is a favorite in France during the fall and winter. Try it with crusty bread and a green salad and you'll see why. This soothing soup will warm your heart and soul. I like to make it with homemade chicken stock, but low-sodium canned broth works, too.

MAKES 6 TO 8 SERVINGS

6 cups chicken broth
3 star anise pods (see note)
2 tablespoons extra-virgin olive oil
2 cups sliced baby leeks
2 cups peeled and cubed Yukon
  Gold potatoes
1 pound roasted chestnuts, peeled
¼ cup dry sherry
½ cup heavy cream
¼ cup fresh Italian parsley leaves,
  chopped
Sea salt and freshly ground black
  pepper
½ cup roasted chestnuts, sliced
  (garnish)
½ cup sour cream or crème fraîche
  (garnish, see note)
½ teaspoon dried culinary
  'Provence' lavender buds
  (garnish)

Bring the broth and star anise to a boil in a medium saucepan over medium-high heat. Reduce the heat to medium-low and simmer for 30 minutes. Remove and discard the star anise.

Warm the oil in a large pot over medium heat. Add the leeks and sauté for 5 minutes, or until translucent. Add the potatoes, chestnuts, and broth. Simmer for 20 minutes, or until the potatoes and chestnuts are tender. Add the sherry and simmer for 5 minutes.

Using a handheld blender or a food processor (work in batches), blend the soup until smooth. Add the cream and parsley. Season with salt and pepper. Return the soup to a gentle simmer.

Serve garnished with sliced chestnuts, a dollop of sour cream or crème fraîche, and a sprinkle of lavender buds.

Star anise is a star-shaped brown pod with an anise flavor. It's used in five-spice powder and a lot of Chinese dishes. Look for it in the spice aisle of large supermarkets.

Crème fraîche is a rich, thickened cream with a slightly tangy flavor. Look for it in upscale supermarkets or make your own, with or without lavender (see page 21).

Beet, Apple, and Carrot Salad
with Lavender Lemon Dressing

Beets and carrots bring lots of appealing color to this winter salad. If you roast the beets ahead of time, it's a quick salad to prepare.

MAKES 6 TO 8 SERVINGS

Lavender Lemon Dressing
   (recipe follows)
1 bunch baby beets, oven roasted
   and peeled (see note)
3 carrots, shredded
2 large Granny Smith apples,
   cored and sliced
2 tablespoons chopped Preserved
   Lavender Lemons (page 22)
1 large head butter lettuce
3 tablespoons fresh Italian parsley
   leaves, chopped

Prepare the dressing.

Cut the beets into wedges and place in a large bowl. Add the carrots, apples, and lemon. Toss to combine. Add the dressing and toss well. Serve at room temperature on a bed of the lettuce. Sprinkle with the parsley.

To roast beets, rinse, rub with olive oil, and trim the stems to 1 inch. Wrap tightly in a large sheet of foil. Place on a baking sheet and roast at 375°F for 30 to 45 minutes, or until tender when tested with a sharp knife. Let cool slightly and slip off the skins.

Lavender Lemon Dressing

¾ cup extra-virgin olive oil
¼ cup white wine vinegar
2 tablespoons fresh lemon juice
¼ cup finely chopped fresh herbs,
   such as thyme, marjoram, basil,
   and parsley
2 teaspoons dried culinary
   'Provence' lavender buds, finely
   ground in a spice grinder
1 large garlic clove, minced
Sea salt and freshly ground black
   pepper

In a small bowl, whisk together the oil, vinegar, lemon juice, herbs, lavender, and garlic. Season with salt and pepper.

Mediterranean Orange and Lemon Salad
with Lavender Vinaigrette

Make this crisp citrus salad in the dead of winter and it'll transport you to the Mediterranean. Close your eyes and imagine you're on a terrace high above the Riviera with the sea below and the breezes softly blowing.

MAKES 8 SERVINGS

2 romaine lettuce hearts
½ cucumber, thinly sliced
½ sweet red onion, slivered
1 medium orange, peeled and
    thinly sliced
1 medium lemon, peeled and
    thinly sliced
Lavender Vinaigrette
    (recipe follows)

Tear the lettuce into bite-size pieces and place on a platter. Scatter the cucumber, onion, orange, and lemon over the lettuce.

Prepare the vinaigrette and pour over the salad. Mix lightly.

Lavender Vinaigrette

⅔ cup extra-virgin olive oil
⅓ cup balsamic vinegar
½ teaspoon sea salt
½ teaspoon dried culinary
    'Provence' lavender buds, finely
    ground in a spice grinder

In a small bowl, whisk together the oil, vinegar, salt, and lavender.

Pacific Northwest Coleslaw
with Spicy Lavender Dressing

What could be prettier than green cabbage dotted with red dried cranberries and crunchy toasted pecans? With its piquant lavender dressing, this isn't a shy slaw. Each bite bursts with flavors of the Pacific Northwest.

MAKES 6 TO 8 SERVINGS

Candied Pecans (recipe follows)
Spicy Lavender Dressing
    (recipe follows)
6 cups shredded green cabbage
3 cups shredded red cabbage
2 cups sweetened dried cranberries,
    chopped
2 Granny Smith apples, cored
    and julienned
1 large yellow bell pepper, julienned
1 large red bell pepper, julienned

Prepare the candied pecans.

Prepare the dressing.

In a large bowl, combine the green cabbage, red cabbage, cranberries, apples, yellow pepper, and red pepper. Add the dressing and toss well. Transfer to a serving platter and sprinkle with the pecans.

Candied Pecans

1 tablespoon unsalted butter
¼ cup pecans, coarsely chopped
2 teaspoons sugar
Pinch of sea salt

Melt the butter in a medium skillet over medium heat. Add the pecans and sauté for 4 minutes, or until lightly toasted. Add the sugar and salt and stir for 1 minute, or until the pecans are well coated. Set aside to cool.

SPICY LAVENDER DRESSING

I teaspoon coriander seeds

I teaspoon cumin seeds

2 teaspoons dried culinary
  'Provence' lavender buds

I cup mayonnaise

¼ cup fresh lemon juice

3 tablespoons fresh lime juice

2 tablespoons maple syrup

I tablespoon malt vinegar

I tablespoon Worcestershire sauce

I tablespoon Dijon mustard

I tablespoon apple cider jelly

4 shallots, minced

I Anaheim chile pepper, chopped

I jalapeño pepper, minced

3 tablespoons minced onion

2 tablespoons fresh cilantro leaves,
  minced

2 tablespoons fresh Italian parsley
  leaves, minced

2 garlic cloves, minced

Sea salt and freshly ground black
  pepper

Toast the coriander and cumin seeds in a dry skillet over medium heat until fragrant, about 2 minutes. Transfer to a spice grinder and add the lavender. Pulse until finely ground. Transfer to the bowl of a food processor.

Add the mayonnaise, lemon juice, lime juice, maple syrup, vinegar, Worcestershire sauce, mustard, jelly, shallots, Anaheim pepper, jalapeño, onion, cilantro, parsley, and garlic. Pulse until smooth and creamy. Transfer to a bowl and season with salt and pepper.

Lavender Lemon Pork Chops
with Caramelized Pears

Pork is a light and tasty meat that's enhanced by the sweetness of pears, figs, and citrus. Lavender and thyme impart a tantalizing taste of the Mediterranean. Served with your favorite winter vegetables, this is a sumptuous late-season dish. Don't be daunted by the lengthy ingredient list, for the technique is simple and straightforward.

MAKES 12 SERVINGS

Mustard Spice Rub (recipe follows)
12 pork loin chops, 1 inch thick
Lavender Lemon Marinade
  (recipe follows)
4 firm but ripe Anjou pears,
  peeled, cored, and cut into
  thick wedges (see note)
½ cup soft dried figs
½ cup sugar
⅓ cup pear nectar or apple juice
1 teaspoon dried thyme
¼ cup sliced almonds, toasted

Prepare the spice rub and rub into the chops on both sides. Place in a large bowl. Cover and refrigerate for at least 1 hour or up to 4 hours.

Prepare the marinade. Measure out 1 cup of marinade and refrigerate until needed. Pour the remainder over the pork and turn to coat all sides. Cover and refrigerate for 8 hours or overnight, turning the pork occasionally.

Preheat the oven to 375°F.

Transfer the pork to a roasting pan large enough to hold the chops in a single layer; discard the marinade. Surround the pork with the pears and figs. Roast for 20 to 25 minutes, or until an instant-read thermometer inserted in the thickest part of a chop registers 150°F.

Transfer the pork and fruit to a platter and tent with foil to keep warm. Pour the pan juices into a small bowl and skim off any fat.

Place the sugar in a large skillet and cook over medium-high heat until the sugar melts and becomes mahogany in color. Do not stir; just gently swirl the melted sugar in the pan to evenly color the syrup. (*Caution:* The sugar syrup is very hot and can burn, so be careful.)

Whisk in the pan juices, pear nectar or apple juice, thyme, and the reserved 1 cup marinade. Whisk over medium-high heat for 10 minutes, or until reduced to a thick sauce.

Pour the sauce over the pork and sprinkle with the almonds.

Anjou pears have yellow-green skin that's often blushed with red. They stay firm and hold together when cooked. They're perfect for dessert as well as savory dishes like this.

MUSTARD SPICE RUB

1 tablespoon cumin seeds, toasted
2 tablespoons brown mustard seeds
1½ tablespoons coarse sea salt
1 tablespoon freshly ground black
  pepper
¾ teaspoon anise seeds
5 or 6 juniper berries

Toast the cumin seeds in a dry skillet over medium heat until fragrant, about 2 minutes. Transfer to a spice grinder and add the mustard seeds, salt, pepper, anise seeds, and juniper berries. Pulse until finely ground.

LAVENDER LEMON MARINADE

½ cup port wine
¼ cup lavender vinegar or white
  wine vinegar
1 tablespoon grated lemon zest
¼ cup fresh lemon juice
1 tablespoon grated orange zest
¼ cup fresh orange juice
1 tablespoon Dijon mustard
¼ cup finely chopped shallot
6 slices Preserved Lavender
  Lemons, finely chopped
  (page 22, optional)
1 tablespoon grated fresh ginger
1 tablespoon dried culinary
  'Provence' lavender buds, finely
  ground in a spice grinder
3 medium garlic cloves, minced
2 fresh thyme sprigs
1 bay leaf

In a small bowl, mix the port, vinegar, lemon zest, lemon juice, orange zest, orange juice, mustard, shallot, lemon (if using), ginger, lavender, garlic, thyme, and bay leaf.

Dude Ranch Beef Stew with Lavender Dumplings

Spices, vegetables, and beef—with a hint of whiskey and lavender—make this a real crowd-pleasing, tummy-filling meal.

MAKES 8 SERVINGS

- 1 (4-pound) eye of round or rump beef roast, well trimmed
- ¾ cup all-purpose flour
- 5 teaspoons dried culinary 'Provence' lavender buds, finely ground in a spice grinder
- 1 teaspoon sea salt
- 1 teaspoon freshly ground black pepper
- ¼ cup plus 3 tablespoons extra-virgin olive oil
- 1 ounce pancetta, finely chopped
- 2 white onions, halved and sliced lengthwise
- 1 leek, cut in half lengthwise and diced (white and pale green parts only)
- 1 tablespoon minced garlic
- 4 cups canned beef broth
- ¼ cup bourbon (see note)
- 1 tablespoon beef demi-glace (see note, optional)
- 1 bouquet garni (see note)
- ¼ teaspoon dried thyme
- 1 orange
- 3 carrots, cut into 1-inch pieces
- ¾ pound fingerling potatoes, cut into ½-inch pieces
- Lavender Dumplings (recipe follows)
- ½ pound small brown mushrooms, quartered
- 1 cup frozen pearl onions, thawed
- 2 tablespoons fresh Italian parsley leaves, chopped

Preheat the oven to 350°F.

Cut the beef into 1½-inch cubes. In a shallow dish, mix the flour, 2 teaspoons of the lavender, salt, and pepper. Dredge the cubes in the flour and shake off the excess.

Heat ¼ cup of the oil in a Dutch oven or other large ovenproof pot over medium heat. Working in batches, cook the beef (stirring occasionally and scraping up the browned bits) for 8 minutes, or until the cubes are beginning to brown. Transfer to a large bowl.

Add the pancetta and the remaining 3 tablespoons oil to the pot. Sauté for 3 minutes. Add the white onions, leek, and garlic. Sauté for 5 minutes. Return the beef to the pot.

In a small bowl, mix the broth and bourbon. Pour into the pot. Cook over medium heat, scraping up any browned bits. Stir in the demi-glace (if using). Simmer for 5 minutes. Add the bouquet garni, thyme, and the remaining 3 teaspoons lavender. Using a vegetable peeler, remove the zest from the orange in a very long strip. Add the strip to the pot; reserve the orange for another use.

Cover and bake, stirring occasionally, for 1½ to 2 hours, or until the beef is just tender.

Add the carrots and potatoes. Cover and bake for 30 to 45 minutes, until the vegetables are just tender.

Prepare the dumpling dough.

Transfer the pot back to the stove. Remove the bouquet garni.

Bring the stew to a simmer over medium heat and add the mushrooms and pearl onions. Gently drop rounded tablespoons of the dough into the stew. Reduce the temperature to low and simmer uncovered for 10 minutes. Cover tightly and cook for 10 minutes, or until the dumplings are puffed and firm to the touch and a skewer pushed into the center of one comes out clean. Serve sprinkled with the parsley.

Safety hint: With a gas range and a hot pot, you have the potential for a flare-up when you add any high-alcohol liquid, such as bourbon. To reduce the risk in this recipe, mix the whiskey with the beef broth first, which dilutes the alcohol percentage.

Demi-glace is a very flavorful, reduced stock. It's available at many butcher shops and specialty food shops as well as from www.morethangourmet.com.

To make a bouquet garni: Combine 8 thyme sprigs, 1 parsley sprig, 1 rosemary sprig, and 2 bay leaves in a square of cheesecloth. Tie with kitchen string. Or look for jars of bouquet garni at upscale food markets.

LAVENDER DUMPLINGS

1½ cups all-purpose flour
¼ cup grated Parmesan cheese
1 tablespoon baking powder
¾ teaspoon sea salt
1 large egg
1 large egg yolk
About ½ cup milk
2 green onions, finely chopped
1 teaspoon dried culinary
    'Provence' lavender buds, finely
    ground in a spice grinder
1 teaspoon fresh lemon thyme or
    thyme leaves

In a large bowl, mix the flour, cheese, baking powder, and salt. In a glass measuring cup, whisk the egg and yolk until blended. Add enough milk to make ¾ cup and whisk to blend. Pour over the dry ingredients. Add the green onions, lavender, and thyme. Mix until just combined.

Lavender Fireside Lamb Stew
with Rosemary and Sage

Here's an unexpected treat for a cold winter's night! Invite friends, add a salad and a loaf of crusty herb bread, and then relax in the warmth of good company and good food. Expect lots of smiles and good cheer. For an even heartier meal, serve the stew over rice.

MAKES 6 SERVINGS

½ cup extra-virgin olive oil

4 large onions, diced

4 celery ribs, thickly sliced

3 large garlic cloves, minced

1½ tablespoons chopped fresh
    rosemary leaves

1½ tablespoons chopped fresh
    sage leaves

4 pounds lamb stew meat, well
    trimmed

Sea salt and freshly ground black
    pepper

⅓ cup all-purpose flour

1 cup dry white wine

1 (14½-ounce) can diced tomatoes,
    with juice

2 carrots, halved lengthwise and
    cut into 1-inch pieces

1 teaspoon dried culinary
    'Provence' lavender buds, finely
    ground in a spice grinder

1 tablespoon Glace de Poulet Gold
    (see note, optional)

2 cups chicken broth

1 (15½-ounce) can garbanzo beans,
    rinsed and drained

Warm ¼ cup of the oil in a large pot over medium-low heat. Add the onions, celery, garlic, 1 tablespoon of the rosemary, and 1 tablespoon of the sage. Sauté for 30 minutes, or until the vegetables are tender but not brown. Remove from the heat.

Cut the lamb into 1½-inch cubes and season with salt and pepper. Place the flour in a shallow dish. Dredge the cubes in the flour and shake off the excess.

Warm the remaining ¼ cup oil in a Dutch oven or other large ovenproof pot over medium heat. Working in batches, cook the lamb for 8 minutes, or until browned. Transfer to a large bowl.

Add the wine to the pot and bring to a boil, scraping up any browned bits. Return the lamb to the pot and bring back to a boil. Reduce the heat to low and simmer for 15 to 20 minutes, or until the liquid is reduced by half.

Preheat the oven to 350°F.

Add the tomatoes to the lamb and boil for 10 minutes. Stir in the carrots, onion mixture, and lavender. Add the glace de poulet (if using) and enough broth to cover the meat and vegetables. Cover the pot and bake for 1 hour and 15 minutes, or until the lamb is tender.

Stir in the beans and bake uncovered for 15 minutes, or until the lamb is very tender and the sauce thickens slightly. (Can be made 1 day ahead up to this point. Cool, cover, and refrigerate. Bring to a simmer before continuing.) Stir the remaining ½ tablespoon rosemary and ½ tablespoon sage into the stew. Season with salt and pepper.

Glace de Poulet Gold is a chicken-stock concentrate. It enriches the flavor of regular broth or stock. You can find this product at most upscale supermarkets and specialty food stores or at www.morethangourmet.com.

Lavender Chicken Chili
with White Beans

This white chili is a nice change from meat and tomato versions. Chicken, white beans, and lavender create a very different dish that will warm you in the middle of winter. It's great for a Super Bowl party.

MAKES 8 SERVINGS

1 pound dried great Northern
    beans, rinsed and picked over
2 pounds boneless, skinless
    chicken breasts, diced
1 tablespoon extra-virgin olive oil
1 pound ground chicken
2 medium white onions, diced
4 garlic cloves, minced
1 tablespoon chopped canned
    jalapeño pepper, with juice
1 tablespoon ground cumin
1 tablespoon dried culinary
    'Provence' lavender buds, finely
    ground in a spice grinder
$1\frac{1}{2}$ teaspoons dried oregano
1 teaspoon dried marjoram
$\frac{1}{2}$ teaspoon ground savory
$\frac{1}{4}$ teaspoon cayenne pepper
6 cups chicken broth
3 cups grated white Cheddar cheese
Sea salt and freshly ground black
    pepper
Sour cream
Fresh tomato salsa or Red Onion
    Lime Salsa (page 170)
Fresh cilantro sprigs

Place the beans in a large bowl and add enough cold water to cover by at least 3 inches. Soak overnight.

Place the diced chicken in a large pot. Add cold water to cover and bring to a simmer over medium heat. Cook for 15 minutes, or until just tender. Drain and set aside to cool.

In the same pot, warm the oil over medium-high heat. Add the ground chicken and onions. Sauté for 10 minutes, or until the onions are translucent. Stir in the garlic and then the jalapeño, cumin, lavender, oregano, marjoram, savory, and cayenne. Sauté for 2 minutes.

Drain the beans and add to the pot. Add the broth and bring to a boil. Reduce the heat and simmer, stirring occasionally, for 2 hours, or until the beans are very tender. Add the diced chicken and 1 cup of the cheese. Stir until the cheese melts. Season with salt and pepper. Serve with the sour cream, salsa, cilantro, and the remaining cheese.

To soak dried beans quickly, rinse and place in a large pot. Cover with 2 inches of cold water. Bring to a boil over high heat. Cover, reduce the heat to medium, and simmer for 10 minutes. Remove from the heat and let stand for $1\frac{1}{2}$ hours. Drain and rinse.

Roasted Lavender Chicken
with Roasted Shallots and Carrots

This robust chicken and vegetable dish is full of the rich, distinctive flavors of Provence. It feeds a crowd and leaves no one hungry. Just add a green salad to whet the appetite and some rustic bread to sop up the juices.

MAKES 8 SERVINGS

Chicken
¾ cup dry white wine
¼ cup grated lemon zest
¼ cup lavender honey or honey
¼ cup Dijon mustard
¼ cup extra-virgin olive oil
1 tablespoon cracked black
    peppercorns
1½ teaspoons fresh lemon juice
1 teaspoon sea salt
½ teaspoon dried culinary
    'Provence' lavender buds, finely
    ground in a spice grinder
8 boneless chicken breast halves
    with skin

Vegetables
Sea salt
2 pounds baby carrots
½ pound shallots, peeled and cut
    in half
2 garlic heads, separated into
    cloves and peeled
1 tablespoon fresh thyme leaves
1 teaspoon lavender honey or honey
1 cup chicken broth
2 tablespoons Glace de Poulet Gold
    (see note, optional)
Fresh lavender sprigs (garnish)

To make the chicken: In a large bowl, mix the wine, lemon zest, honey, mustard, oil, pepper, lemon juice, salt, and lavender. Add the chicken and turn to coat. Cover and refrigerate for 4 hours.

To make the vegetables: Preheat the oven to 350°F.

Bring about half a pot of water to a boil in a large saucepan. Season with salt and add the carrots. Boil for 5 minutes, then drain. Transfer to a bowl of ice water to cool; drain.

In a large bowl, mix the carrots, shallots, garlic, thyme, and honey. Transfer to a large roasting pan. Remove the chicken from the marinade and place on top of the vegetables; discard the remaining marinade.

Mix the broth and glace de poulet (if using). Pour half into the roasting pan. Roast, basting frequently, for 45 minutes, or until the chicken is no longer pink when tested with a sharp knife and the skin is nicely browned. Add extra stock as necessary while basting. Transfer the chicken to the center of a platter and surround with the vegetables. Garnish with lavender sprigs.

Glace de Poulet Gold is a chicken-stock concentrate. It enriches the flavor of regular broth or stock. You can find this product at most upscale supermarkets and specialty food stores or at www.morethangourmet.com.

SOUTHWESTERN SALISBURY STEAKS
WITH RED ONION LIME SALSA

The humble cube steak goes gourmet! This quick and easy dish features lavender and flavors of the Southwest. Serve with Mashed Sweet Potatoes with Lavender and Lime (page 176).

MAKES 6 SERVINGS

Red Onion Lime Salsa
    (recipe follows)
4 bacon slices, cut into ¼-inch
    pieces
½ cup plus 2 tablespoons
    all-purpose flour
2 teaspoons chili powder
1 teaspoon dried culinary
    'Provence' lavender buds, finely
    ground in a spice grinder
6 beef cube steaks, about 4 ounces
    each
Sea salt and freshly ground black
    pepper
3 tablespoons unsalted butter
2 medium red onions, diced
2 tablespoons minced garlic
½ cup canned chopped mild green
    chile peppers
2 tablespoons minced green onion
1 cup beef broth
¼ cup tequila
½ cup shredded Monterey Jack
    cheese
¼ cup fresh cilantro leaves,
    chopped
1 avocado, halved, pitted, peeled,
    and sliced
Fresh cilantro sprigs

Prepare the salsa.

Preheat the oven to 350°F.

Cook the bacon in a large skillet over medium-high heat until crisp. Using a slotted spoon, transfer the bacon to a bowl.

Place ½ cup of the flour in a shallow bowl and mix in the chili powder and lavender. Season the steaks with salt and pepper. Dip them into the flour to coat and shake off the excess. Cook the steaks in the bacon fat over medium heat for 3 minutes per side, or until browned. Transfer to a roasting pan in a single layer.

Add the butter, red onions, and garlic to the skillet. Cook for 5 minutes, or until very soft and caramelized around the edges. Stir in the chile peppers, green onion, and the remaining 2 tablespoons flour. Stir over low heat for 2 minutes. Mix the broth and tequila and stir into the skillet. Stir for 5 minutes, or until smooth and thickened.

Pour over the steaks and sprinkle with the bacon, cheese, and chopped cilantro. Bake for 35 minutes, or until tender.

Transfer to a platter and top with the avocado slices and cilantro sprigs. Serve with the salsa.

Red Onion Lime Salsa

2 medium red onions, thinly sliced

Grated zest of 1 lime

¼ cup fresh lime juice

2 tablespoons fresh cilantro leaves, chopped

2 tablespoons extra-virgin olive oil

1 teaspoon chili powder

½ teaspoon dried oregano

½ teaspoon fresh lemon thyme or thyme leaves

½ teaspoon sea salt

In a large bowl, mix the onions, lime zest, lime juice, cilantro, oil, chili powder, oregano, thyme, and salt. Cover and refrigerate for at least 1 hour or up to 1 day.

STUFFED BREAST OF TURKEY ALLA FLORENTINE

Sometimes we like to try something different. This excellent new way to serve turkey retains many of the flavors we associate with a traditional holiday dinner. The presentation is elegant and perfect for a festive gathering. You'll want this recipe in your holiday file.

MAKES 6 TO 8 SERVINGS

Florentine Stuffing (recipe follows)
1 (3½-pound) bone-in turkey
    breast with skin
Sea salt and freshly ground black
    pepper
4 tablespoons unsalted butter
1 tablespoon extra-virgin olive oil
1 medium onion, diced
1 carrot, diced
1 celery rib, diced
3 cups turkey stock or chicken broth
1 cup dry white wine
2 shallots, chopped
1 garlic clove, chopped
1 teaspoon dried culinary
    'Provence' lavender buds, finely
    ground in a spice grinder
1 bouquet garni (page 165)
3 tablespoons all-purpose flour
1 bunch watercress (garnish)

Prepare the stuffing.

Remove the bones from the turkey breast (save them to make stock). Spread the breast, skin side down, on a large sheet of parchment paper. Pound the breast to an even ¼-inch thickness for easier rolling. You'll have a large roughly shaped rectangle. Position it so one of the long sides is facing you.

Sprinkle the turkey with salt and pepper. Spread the stuffing over the meat, leaving a 1-inch border.

Turn in about 2 inches of meat from the left and right sides to keep the stuffing from coming out and also to square off the sides. Starting at the long edge facing you, tightly roll the meat into a log shape to enclose the stuffing. Use kitchen twine to tie the roll at 1-inch intervals so the log holds its shape.

Preheat the oven to 350°F.

Melt 2 tablespoons of the butter in a large skillet over medium heat. Add the oil and then brown the turkey on all sides. Transfer the turkey to a plate. Add the onion, carrot, and celery to the skillet. Cover and cook for 5 minutes, or until softened. Transfer to a shallow roasting pan and place the turkey on top.

Add the stock or broth, wine, shallots, garlic, lavender, and bouquet garni. Season with salt and pepper. Cover with a piece of parchment and then foil. Crimp the edges to seal all around the roasting pan.

Bake for 2 hours.

Transfer the turkey to a cutting board and allow to stand for 20 minutes before slicing. Strain the cooking liquid into a medium saucepan (discard the vegetables). Boil until reduced to about 1½ cups.

Melt the remaining 2 tablespoons butter in a small saucepan over medium heat. Add the flour and whisk until lightly browned. Slowly whisk in the reduced liquid. Continue whisking until slightly thickened. Keep warm over low heat.

Discard the strings from the turkey and carve most of the meat into ⅜-inch slices. Arrange them overlapping on a platter with the uncut piece of turkey at one end. Garnish with the watercress. Pass the gravy separately.

Florentine Stuffing

2 tablespoons unsalted butter

I medium white onion, finely
   chopped

2 small bunches fresh spinach,
   chopped

I pound ground turkey

I cup fresh bread crumbs

½ cup grated Romano cheese

⅓ cup pine nuts, toasted

2 tablespoons fresh Italian parsley
   leaves, chopped

2 garlic cloves, finely chopped

I tablespoon dried culinary
   'Provence' lavender buds, finely
   ground in a spice grinder

Grated zest of I lemon

Pinch of grated nutmeg

Sea salt and freshly ground black
   pepper

2 large eggs, slightly beaten

¼ cup dry white wine

Melt the butter in a large skillet over medium heat. Add the onion and sauté for 5 minutes, or until soft but not brown. Add the spinach and sauté for 2 minutes, or until just wilted. Transfer to a large bowl and let cool for 10 minutes.

Add the ground turkey, bread crumbs, cheese, pine nuts, parsley, garlic, lavender, lemon zest, and nutmeg. Season with salt and pepper. Stir in the eggs and wine. Mix well.

To be sure your stuffing is perfectly seasoned, mix it and then sauté a teaspoonful in a little oil. Taste and adjust the seasonings if needed.

Polenta Tart with Cremini Mushrooms

A hearty and yet luxurious dish, this savory mushroom tart is equally good as a side dish, an appetizer, or the centerpiece of a luncheon (accompanied by a salad). This is a variation of a recipe from my friend Peggy Fallon, a culinary instructor who taught an appetizer class at Mon Chéri Cooking School.

MAKES 8 TO 10 SERVINGS

Polenta

2 cups milk

2 cups chicken broth

½ teaspoon dried culinary
   'Provence' lavender buds, finely
   ground in a spice grinder

½ teaspoon sea salt

I cup polenta

½ cup grated Parmesan cheese

4 tablespoons unsalted butter

Mushrooms

4 tablespoons unsalted butter

3 large shallots, finely chopped

½ pound cremini mushrooms,
   thinly sliced

2 tablespoons all-purpose flour

½ cup heavy cream

3 tablespoons chopped chives

2 tablespoons fresh Italian parsley
   leaves, chopped

I½ teaspoons fresh thyme leaves

½ teaspoon dried thyme

½ teaspoon dried culinary
   'Provence' lavender buds, finely
   ground in a spice grinder

½ teaspoon fresh lemon juice

½ teaspoon sea salt

To make the polenta: In the top of a double boiler or a metal bowl that fits atop a saucepan, combine the milk, broth, lavender, and salt. Cook over simmering water until steaming. Gradually whisk in the polenta. Cook, stirring very frequently, for about 45 minutes, or until thick and creamy. Whisk in the cheese and butter.

To make the mushrooms: Melt the butter in a large skillet over medium heat. Add the shallots and cook for 5 minutes, or until softened but not browned. Stir in the mushrooms and cook for 10 minutes, or until all the moisture they release has evaporated. Sprinkle with the flour and stir for 2 minutes. Stir in the cream and bring to a boil. Remove from the heat and stir in the chives, parsley, fresh thyme, dried thyme, lavender, lemon juice, and salt.

Line a 9- or 10-inch fluted tart pan with plastic wrap. Fill with half of the polenta. Spread the mushrooms over the polenta in an even layer. Top with the remaining polenta. Cover with plastic wrap and refrigerate for 2 hours, or until firm. (This will keep for several days refrigerated.)

Preheat the oven to 400°F.

Remove the top sheet of plastic wrap and invert the tart onto a parchment-lined or nonstick baking sheet. Remove the bottom plastic wrap. Bake the tart for 15 minutes, or until heated through.

Polenta loves to be stirred. The creamiest polenta is stirred well and often.

After baking, the tart can be decorated with extra cooked mushrooms or sprigs of fresh lavender.

Lavender Roasted Beets
with Garlic and Lemon

Beets are naturally high in sugar, and roasting intensifies their sweetness. Here, lemon, garlic, and lavender combine magically with the earthy-sweet beets. Serve this colorful vegetable with roasted lavender chicken and buttered green beans.

MAKES 6 SERVINGS

1 pound medium beets, with 1 inch of stems remaining
6 unpeeled garlic cloves
¼ cup plus 1 tablespoon extra-virgin olive oil
1 tablespoon plus ½ teaspoon dried culinary 'Provence' lavender buds, finely ground in a spice grinder
¼ teaspoon finely grated lemon zest
2 tablespoons fresh lemon juice
Sea salt and freshly ground black pepper
¼ cup Italian parsley leaves, chopped

Preheat the oven to 375°F.

Place the beets and garlic on a large sheet of foil and sprinkle with ¼ cup of the oil and 1 tablespoon of the lavender; toss to combine. Fold up the foil to make a sealed packet. Place on a baking sheet. Roast for 30 to 45 minutes, or until tender when tested with a sharp knife. Set aside until cool enough to handle. Slip off the skins.

Cut the beets into quarters and place in a large skillet. Squeeze the garlic over the beets. Stir in the lemon zest, lemon juice, the remaining 1 tablespoon oil, and the remaining ½ teaspoon lavender. Season with salt and pepper. Warm through over medium heat. Sprinkle with the parsley. Serve hot or warm.

The beets can be prepared up to 1 day ahead and refrigerated. Rewarm before serving.

RISOTTO-STYLE YUKON GOLD POTATOES
WITH LAVENDER AND ROSEMARY

This dish was done at the Ahwahnee Hotel in Yosemite by guest chef Pierre Albaladejo. He took the Italian way of making risotto and adapted it to potatoes instead of arborio rice. I further enhanced the recipe by adding lavender.

MAKES 8 SERVINGS

1 cup milk
1 cup chicken broth
2 tablespoons extra-virgin olive oil
1 medium onion, chopped
2 teaspoons dried culinary 'Provence' lavender buds, finely ground in a spice grinder
½ teaspoon chopped fresh rosemary leaves
1 garlic clove, minced
6 large Yukon Gold potatoes, peeled and finely diced
½ cup grated Parmesan cheese
2 tablespoons unsalted butter
Sea salt and freshly ground black pepper

Combine the milk and broth in a small saucepan. Bring just to a simmer over medium heat. Keep warm over low heat.

Warm the oil in a large skillet over medium-high heat. Add the onion and sauté for 5 minutes, or until translucent. Add the lavender, rosemary, and garlic. Sauté for 30 seconds. Add the potatoes and sauté for 2 minutes. Slowly pour in the warm milk and bring to a simmer, stirring constantly.

Reduce the heat to medium and cook, stirring often, for 20 minutes, or until the potatoes are very tender and the liquid has become very thick and creamy. Stir in the cheese and butter. Season with salt and pepper.

Mashed Sweet Potatoes
with Lavender and Lime

Adding lime and lavender to sweet potatoes creates a whole new winter taste treat! I suggest serving this with Southwestern Salisbury Steaks with Red Onion Lime Salsa (page 169). For something just slightly different, use Yukon Gold potatoes as a substitute.

This may be made up to 2 days ahead and refrigerated. Reheat in a microwave for 1 minute before serving.

MAKES 6 SERVINGS

2 pounds Jewel sweet potatoes
   (see note)
¼ pound (1 stick) unsalted butter,
   melted
¼ cup fresh lime juice
½ teaspoon dried culinary
   'Provence' lavender buds, finely
   ground in a spice grinder
Sea salt and freshly ground black
   pepper
Chopped fresh cilantro leaves
Grated zest of 1 lime

Preheat the oven to 400°F.

Prick the sweet potatoes several times with a fork. Place on a foil-lined baking sheet and bake for 1 hour, or until very soft. Set aside until cool enough to handle.

Scoop the flesh into a bowl; discard the skins. Using a handheld blender or a food processor, blend until smooth. Stir in the butter, lime juice, and lavender. Season with salt and pepper. Sprinkle with the cilantro and lime zest.

Jewel is a "yam-type" sweet potato, which means it's moist and sweet when baked. It has light copper skin and orange flesh.

Honey Lavender Pound Cake
with White Chocolate Drizzle

This rich cake is imbued with lustrous flavors that complement each other. Whether you serve it at a tea party or as the finale to a great meal, the lavender-scented cake with its pink-hued white chocolate drizzle will be truly memorable.

MAKES 12 TO 18 SERVINGS

1 tablespoon dried culinary 'Provence' lavender buds, finely ground in a spice grinder

$2^{3}/_{4}$ cups sugar

3 cups cake flour

$^{1}/_{4}$ teaspoon baking soda

1 cup sour cream

$^{1}/_{4}$ cup honey or lavender honey

6 large eggs

$^{1}/_{2}$ teaspoon salt

$^{1}/_{2}$ pound (2 sticks) unsalted butter, at room temperature

1 teaspoon vanilla extract

White Chocolate Drizzle (recipe follows)

Preheat the oven to 350°F. Grease and flour a 10-inch tube pan.

Place the lavender in a spice grinder with 2 tablespoons of the sugar. Pulse until the lavender is finely ground. Transfer to a small bowl and stir in the remaining sugar.

Sift the flour and baking soda together three times.

In a small bowl, mix the sour cream and honey.

Separate the eggs, placing the whites in a large bowl and the yolks in a cup. Add $^{1}/_{4}$ teaspoon of the salt to the whites and beat with an electric mixer until stiff peaks form.

In another large bowl, combine the butter and sugar. Beat with the mixer until fluffy. Beat in the vanilla and the remaining $^{1}/_{4}$ teaspoon salt. Beat in the yolks, one at a time, beating well after each addition.

Beginning with the dry ingredients, alternately beat in the flour and sour cream in three additions each. Fold in the egg whites. Pour into the prepared pan.

Bake for 1 hour, or until a skewer inserted in the center of the cake comes out clean. Let cool for 10 minutes and then invert onto a wire rack. Cool completely.

Prepare the white chocolate drizzle. Use a whisk to drizzle the warm mixture over the cooled cake.

White Chocolate Drizzle

$5^{1}/_{4}$ ounces white chocolate, chopped

1 tablespoon grenadine or Italian pomegranate syrup

1 tablespoon heavy cream

Place the chocolate in the top of a double boiler or a metal bowl that fits atop a saucepan. Stir over simmering water for 2 minutes, or until melted. Whisk in the grenadine or pomegranate syrup and then the cream.

Lavender Devil's Food Cake

This family favorite comes from my mother, Marguerite. She made it as a special treat for her children's birthdays. I enhanced the chocolate cake with lavender and espresso powder for a more grown-up flavor.

For the best results, use a natural-process cocoa powder, such as regular Hershey's. Do not use Dutch-process cocoa for this recipe because it is less acidic. You need the extra acidity to react with the baking powder and give the cake more rising power.

MAKES 8 TO 12 SERVINGS

2 cups all-purpose flour
¼ cup unsweetened natural-process
    cocoa powder, sifted
2 teaspoons dried culinary
    'Provence' lavender buds, finely
    ground in a spice grinder
1½ teaspoons baking soda
1 cup water
½ cup buttermilk or sour milk
    (see note)
¼ pound (1 stick) unsalted butter,
    at room temperature
2 cups sugar
2 large eggs
1 teaspoon vanilla extract
Cocoa Filling (recipe follows)
Chocolate Lavender Frosting
    (recipe follows)
1 cup chopped walnuts

Preheat the oven to 350°F. Grease two 8-inch cake pans and line the bottoms with parchment paper.

Sift the flour, cocoa, lavender, and baking soda into a medium bowl.

In a small bowl, mix the water and buttermilk or sour milk.

Combine the butter and sugar in a large bowl. Beat with an electric mixer until fluffy. Beat in the eggs and vanilla. Beginning with the dry ingredients, alternately beat in the flour and milk in three additions each.

Bake on the center rack for 25 minutes, or until a tester inserted in the center comes out clean and the cake begins to pull away from the sides of the pan. Cool on wire racks for 5 minutes. Run a thin knife around the sides of the pans and invert the cakes onto wire racks. Peel off the paper. Cool completely.

Prepare the cocoa filling.

Prepare the frosting.

Place one cake layer, flat side up, on a 10-inch cardboard round. Spread with the filling. Top with the second cake layer, flat side down. Spread a thin layer of frosting over the top and sides of the cake to seal in any crumbs. Spread the remaining frosting over the top and sides of the cake. (If the frosting becomes stiff as you work, stir gently with a spatula.) Decorate the sides with the walnuts.

Cover with a cake dome and refrigerate for at least 2 hours or up to 2 days. Let stand at room temperature for 1 hour before serving.

To make sour milk, stir 1½ teaspoons vinegar or lemon juice into ½ cup warm milk. Let stand for 5 minutes, until the milk looks curdled.

Cocoa Filling

⅓ cup sugar

4 teaspoons all-purpose flour

1 tablespoon unsweetened cocoa powder

1 cup water

1 tablespoon unsalted butter

½ teaspoon vanilla extract

In a medium saucepan, whisk together the sugar, flour, and cocoa. Slowly whisk in the water. Keep whisking to work out all lumps. Add the butter and place over medium heat. Bring to a boil and whisk constantly. Boil for 3 to 5 minutes, or until the mixture thickly coats the back of a spoon. Add the vanilla and remove from the heat. Let cool to room temperature.

Chocolate Lavender Frosting

6 tablespoons unsalted butter, at room temperature

⅓ cup unsweetened cocoa powder, sifted

1 teaspoon vanilla extract

½ teaspoon espresso powder

½ teaspoon dried culinary 'Provence' lavender buds, finely ground in a spice grinder

2⅔ cups confectioners' sugar

⅓ cup milk

Place the butter in a large bowl and beat with an electric mixer until fluffy. Beat in the cocoa, vanilla, espresso powder, and lavender. Alternately beat in the confectioners' sugar and milk. Beat to spreading consistency, adding more milk if needed.

ROASTED LAVENDER SPICED PEARS
AND DRIED PLUMS WITH ALMONDS

This is one of my favorites! The familiar flavors of cinnamon, allspice, and vanilla go perfectly with the fruit. To dress it up, serve in martini glasses. Try this with Lavender Lemon Cookies (page 94).

MAKES 8 SERVINGS

¾ cup pineapple juice (see note)
4 firm but ripe Anjou pears
4 tablespoons unsalted butter
½ cup sugar
1 teaspoon ground cinnamon
1 vanilla bean, cut in half
    lengthwise
½ pound soft pitted dried plums
    (prunes), quartered
1 tablespoon dried culinary
    'Provence' lavender buds, finely
    ground in a spice grinder
1 cup sliced almonds, toasted
Lavender Crème Fraîche
    (page 21)

Preheat the oven to 450°F. Line a rimmed baking sheet with parchment paper.

Place the pineapple juice in a large bowl. Peel the pears, halve lengthwise, and remove the cores with a melon baller. Slice each half into 3 wedges. As you work, add the pears to the bowl and toss with the juice.

Melt the butter in a large skillet over medium heat. Stir in the sugar and cinnamon. Scrape the vanilla seeds into the skillet and add the rest of the bean. Add the plums and lavender. Drain the pears and add to the skillet. Stir to coat well.

Transfer the mixture to the prepared baking sheet and spread in an even layer. Bake for 15 to 20 minutes, or until the pears are just tender. Remove from the oven and gently stir in ¾ cup of the almonds.

Divide the fruit among dessert bowls. Spoon on some of the pan juices and sprinkle with the remaining ¼ cup almonds. Top with spoonfuls of the crème fraîche.

The pineapple juice keeps the pears from turning brown. Lemon juice would achieve the same result, but the pineapple juice has a milder taste.

California Avocado Cream Pie

Really, you can use avocados to make a creamy, delicious pie! Orange zest and lavender contribute delightful flavor to both the crust and filling.

MAKES 12 SERVINGS

Orange Pastry Crust
   (recipe follows)
³/₄ **cup water**
1 **envelope unflavored gelatin**
1 **teaspoon grated orange zest**
¹/₂ **cup orange juice**
¹/₃ **cup sugar**
2 **teaspoons dried culinary**
   'Provence' lavender buds, finely
   ground in a spice grinder
¹/₄ **teaspoon salt**
2 **large avocados**
2 **tablespoons fresh lemon juice**
1 **cup heavy cream, whipped**

Prepare the crust.

Place the water in a small saucepan and sprinkle with the gelatin. Let stand for 1 minute to soften. Stir over low heat for 2 to 3 minutes, or until the water is warm and the gelatin melts. Add the orange zest, orange juice, sugar, lavender, and salt. Continue stirring until the sugar dissolves. Transfer to a large bowl.

Halve, pit, and peel the avocados. Coarsely chop and place in a medium bowl. Mix in the lemon juice. Using a fork or a potato masher, mash the avocados well. Place a sieve over a bowl and force the avocados through it to make a smooth puree. (Alternatively, blend the chopped avocado in a food processor until smooth.)

Measure out 1 cup of the puree; reserve any remainder for another use. Fold into the gelatin mixture. Fold in the whipped cream.

Pour into the baked crust and refrigerate for at least 3 hours, or until set.

To hasten the ripening of rock-hard avocados, punch several holes in a paper bag and add the avocados plus a small apple. Close the bag and keep at room temperature for 2 days. The apple gives off ethylene gas, which helps ripen the avocados.

Orange Pastry Crust

1²⁄₃ cups all-purpose flour

¹⁄₃ cup sugar

2¹⁄₂ teaspoons dried culinary 'Provence' lavender buds, finely ground in a spice grinder

1 teaspoon baking powder

1 teaspoon grated orange zest

¹⁄₄ teaspoon salt

¹⁄₄ pound (1 stick) cold unsalted butter, cut into small pieces

1 large egg

4 tablespoons ice water

In the bowl of a food processor, combine the flour, sugar, lavender, baking powder, orange zest, and salt. Pulse to mix. Scatter the butter over the flour and pulse until the mixture resembles coarse crumbs; do not overprocess. In a cup, mix the egg and 2 tablespoons of the water. Add to the crumbs and pulse until the dough starts to clump; if the dough is not clumping, add more water 1 tablespoon at a time. Gather the dough into a ball and flatten into a disk. Wrap in plastic wrap. Refrigerate for 1 hour.

Preheat the oven to 375°F.

On a lightly floured surface, roll the dough into a 13-inch round. Fit into a 9-inch pie plate and trim the overhang to about ³⁄₄ inch. Turn under and flute the edges. Chill for about 15 minutes. Line the pie plate with parchment paper. Cover the parchment with dried beans or pie weights. Bake for 12 minutes, or until set and golden brown. Remove beans or weights and bake for another 4 minutes. Cool on a wire rack.

A WEALTH OF
LAVENDER RESOURCES

If you are looking for lavender plants, your best bet is to find a nearby grower or reputable nursery. You can inspect the plants and will know exactly what you're getting. Buying mail-order plants is more costly and should be done only if you have no other options.

By the same token, it would be nice if you could obtain culinary lavender buds and other supplies locally. Nothing beats instant gratification—and no shipping charges!

That said, the following establishments carry a wonderful selection of lavender products. If you're lucky enough to live near them, take advantage of your good fortune. Otherwise, they're just a phone call or e-mail away.

Dried Culinary Lavender Buds, Plants, and Seeds

Rancho Alegre Lavender (herb farm; organic dried culinary 'Provence' lavender buds)
413 Dearborn Park Road
Pescadero, CA 94060
Phone: 650-879-1876
www.ranchoalegre-lavender.com
E-mail: susanditz@earthlink.net

Mon Chéri Cooking School & Caterers (organic dried culinary 'Provence' lavender buds, Lavender Ginger Seasoning, Lavender Chile Seasoning, and other lavender food products)
461 South Murphy Avenue
Sunnyvale, CA 94086
Phone: 408-736-0892
Fax: 408-736-0932
www.moncheriicookingschool.com
E-mail: sship25521@aol.com

For the Love of Lavender (organic culinary lavender buds; jams, marmalades, and chutneys made with lavender. Lavender and complimentary herbs in bath and body care, home accessories, culinary and plant materials.)
PO Box 31580
Santa Fe, NM 87594
Phone: 505.424.9199
FAX: 505.424.8991
www.fortheoflavender.net
Email: rhmurray@comcast.net

Jardin du Soleil Lavender Farm (Dried lavender buds, and lavender products)
3932 Sequim-Dungeness Way
Sequim, WA 98382
Phone: 360 582-1185
www.jardindusoleil.com

Dean & DeLuca (dried culinary lavender buds)
Phone: 877-826-9246
Fax: 800-781-4050
www.deandeluca.com

Lavandula Lavender Farm (culinary lavender buds, farm tours, events, and market)
P.O. Box 35
Hepburn Springs 3461, Australia
Phone: 03-5476-4393
Fax: 03-5476-4390
www.lavandula.com.au

Lavender Creek Farm (organic dried culinary 'Provence' lavender buds; lavender luncheons and tours; pick your own lavender)
32379 Route 9
Mackinaw, IL 61755
Phone: 309-359-5555
www.lavendercreekfarm.com

LavenderFarms.com
An online consortium of Olympic Peninsula
    (Washington State) lavender growers
www.lavenderfarms.com

Musée de la Lavande (lavender museum and market)
Route de Gordes
84220 Coustellet, France
Phone: 04-90-76-91-23
Fax: 04-90-76-85-52
www.museedelalavande.com

Richters Herb Specialists (nonculinary lavender
    and culinary lavender herb seeds)
P.O. Box 26
Goodwood, Ontario L0C 1A0
Phone: 905-640-6677
Fax: 905-640-6641
www.richters.com

Whole Foods Markets (dried culinary lavender buds)
www.wholefoods.com/stores/index.html

Specialty Ingredients Made with Lavender

Arnabal International (lavender vinegar)
13459 Savanna
Tustin, CA 92782
Phone/fax: 714-665-9477
E-mail: arnabal@pacbell.net
www.arnabal.com

Green Emporium Restaurant/Gallery (restaurant
    offering lavender food menu and lavender
    products sold at restaurant and online)
P.O. Box 311
Colrain, MA 01340
Phone: 413-624-5122
www.lavenderlovers.com

Mon Chéri Cooking School & Caterers (organic dried
    culinary 'Provence' lavender buds, Lavender Ginger
    Seasoning, Lavender Chile Seasoning, and other
    lavender food products)
461 South Murphy Avenue
Sunnyvale, CA 94086
Phone: 408-736-0892
Fax: 408-736-0932
www.monchericookingschool.com
E-mail: sship25521@aol.com

Murchies Tea & Coffee Ltd. (black lavender tea)
5580 Parkwood Way
Richmond, British Columbia V6V 2M4
Phone: 800-663-0400
www.murchies.com/home.html

Taylor Maid Farms (black lavender tea)
6793 McKinley Street
Sebastopol, CA 95472
Phone: 888-688-7272
Fax: 707-824-0715
www.taylormaidfarms.com

Other Culinary Resources

The Baker's Catalogue (decorative baking sugar and
    baking equipment)
P.O. Box 876
Norwich, Vermont 05055-0876
Phone: 800-827-6836
www.bakerscatalogue.com

The Bridge Company (pans, cooking equipment,
    and tools)
214 East 52nd Street
New York, NY 10022
Phone: 212-688-4220
www.bridgekitchenware.com

Dean & DeLuca (Asian culinary supplies and
pomegranate molasses)
Phone: 877-826-9246
Fax: 800-781-4050
www.deandeluca.com

India Tree Gourmet Spices & Specialties (decorative
baking sugar)
4240 Gilman Place West #B
Seattle, WA 98199
Phone: 800-369-4848

Los Chileros de Nuevo Mexico (achiote rojo spiced
seasoning paste)
P.O. Box 6215
Santa Fe, NM 87502
Phone: 505-471-6967
www.loschileros.com
E-mail: info@hotchilepepper.com
Marquez Brothers International Inc. (achiote rojo
spiced seasoning paste)
El Mexicano Brand
5801 Rue Ferrari
San Jose, CA 95138
Phone: 408-960-2700
www.marquezbrothers.com

More Than Gourmet (low-salt, meat, and
vegetable stock concentrates)
929 Home Avenue
Akron, OH 44310
Phone: 800-860-9385
www.morethangourmet.com

Orchard Choice, Valley Fig Growers (fig puree)
P.O. Box 1987
Fresno, CA 93718
Phone: 559-237-3893
www.valleyfig.com/shopping/index.html

Sur La Table (cooking equipment and tools)
Phone: 800-243-0852
www.surlatable.com

Lavender Festivals in the United States

Lavender Trail is presented by the Hill Country
Lavender Growers Asso.
Hill Country Tx.
May

Lavender in the Valley
Albuquerque New Mexico
Second Weekend in July

Mantanzas Creek Winery Lavender Festival
Santa Rosa, CA
June

Ojai Lavender Festival
Ojai CA
First Weekend in June

Sequim, Lavender Festival
WA
Third Weekend in July

INDEX